LIVING STORIES
OF FAVORITE SONGS

Living Stories
of Favorite Songs

by

ERNEST K. EMURIAN

Author of

Plays and Pageants for Many Occasions
More Plays and Pageants for Many Occasions
Living Stories of Famous Hymns
Famous Stories of Inspiring Hymns
Stories of our National Songs
Stories of Christmas Carols

Boston   W. A. WILDE COMPANY PUBLISHERS   *Massachusetts*

1083460

To
A Friend

PREFACE

The success of the weekly newspaper column, HYMN OF THE WEEK, which resulted in my recent book, LIVING STORIES OF FAMOUS HYMNS, published in the fall of 1955, encouraged me to continue the series by narrating the stories behind favorite sentimental, railroad, convivial, love, children's, patriotic and state songs, as well as those classified as miscellaneous.

I had been collecting information from many sources over a period of fifteen years, but never actually decided to write this book until the middle of May, 1955. During the weeks from May 11 to June 7, when our family was wondering whether we were to be moved after a very happy eight year pastorate at Elm Ave Methodist Church, Portsmouth, Virginia, to another parish at the session of the Virginia Annual Conference of the Methodist Church, scheduled for the third week in June, I occupied myself writing these thirty-five stories, as much to relieve the inner tension of the preacher as to share this interesting information with the reading public.

I trust those authors and composers who are still alive, and/or their loved ones, relatives and families, will excuse the liberties I took in writing some of the details of several of these stories, in order to bring out salient facts that are somewhat related to the actual history of the song. I will be grateful for their indulgence.

And for those who may be curious, we were not moved to another Church after all, but were returned for our ninth year.

ERNEST K. EMURIAN

Elm Ave Methodist Church
Portsmouth, Va. 1958. Still here.

CONTENTS

7

LIVING STORIES
OF FAVORITE SONGS

1.

CARRY ME BACK TO OLD VIRGINNY

George Primrose, famous soft-shoe dancer and star of Skiff and Gaylord's Minstrel Show, propped his feet up on his dressing table, leaned back in an easy chair and said, "Who was that who wanted to see me, John?"

John Ford, owner of Ford's Theater where the show was enjoying a successful run, replied, "A young man who has a lot of real talent, George."

"You mean to imply that Skiff and Gaylord's world-famous minstrel show is lacking in talent?" the entertainer asked.

"Nothing of the sort," the owner of the theater replied. "But everyone knows that you and Billy West are planning to leave and join up with Colonel Haverly's outfit."

"He promised us top billing if we did, so we're joining up," the black-faced comedian explained.

"In that case we'll be needing some new talent around here. That's why I want you to hear this youngster," Ford continued.

"Well, bring him in," Primrose said. "But first, tell me something about who he is and what he does." Ford took a seat in the crowded dressing room. "Well," he began, "first of all, I met him one night a few weeks ago in Lafayette Square right here in Washington. When I heard him play the banjo and sing one of his own songs, I knew right away he was a natural born artist if I ever heard one."

"How old is he?"

"Nineteen or twenty. And I know his father, too. He's a clerk in the Patent Office."

"What does the boy do?"

"He's a student at Howard University," Ford replied.

11

"Harvard?" Primrose asked, wondering why a university student from Boston would want a part in a show in Washington.

"Not Harvard, George, but Howard, the new government university for Negroes here in Washington," Ford explained.

"You mean he's a colored boy?"

"Yes," Ford continued. "But let me bring him in here anyway. He deserves a break and you may be the one to give it to him."

Primrose turned to another minstrel man who entered the room. "Funny thing," he said, "we black our faces to look colored but we can't have a real colored man in the show. We can blacken our faces and sing their songs but they can't whiten their faces and sing our songs. Why doesn't he try Haverly's Colored Minstrels?"

"Because he idolizes you, George. To him you are the greatest minstrel man in the world, and I'm going to bring him in whether you like it or not," Ford said, leaving the room. He returned a few moments later bringing a slender half-frightened colored youth with him. "This is James A. Bland. Bland, this is George Primrose." After the introductions, Primrose motioned to chairs, and the men sat down as the conversation continued. "Tell us about yourself, James," Primrose said, trying to put the young man at ease.

"Well, Mr. Primrose," Bland began, "I was born in Long Island in '54 as a free American, coming from a long line of emancipated Negroes. My father, Allen Bland, is a graduate of Wilberforce University and has a law degree from Howard, here in Washington. He was the first Negro ever appointed to a government position, and served as an examiner with the United States Post Office for many years. When I was thirteen, I saw an old Negro playing a banjo and singing and I fell in love with music and have been in love with it ever since. I do some entertaining and singing in restaurants and clubs around Washington, to pick up some extra money when I'm not going to school. My folks want me to graduate from Howard, but I want to be a musician and a minstrel man like you, Mr. Primrose."

12

"Interesting, James. Suppose you play me something that you wrote yourself. Ford tells us you're quite talented," Primrose added.

Bland picked up his banjo, struck a few chords, and said, "I wrote this one a few weeks ago." Singing plaintively as he chorded his own accompaniment, Bland began to sing:

Oh, my golden slippers am laid away, Kase I don't spect to wear 'em till my wedding day,
And my long tailed coat dat I loved so well, I will wear up in de chariot in the morn;
And my long white robe dat I bought last June, I'm gwine to get changed kase it fits too soon,
And de old grey hoss dat I used to drive, I will hitch up to de chariot in de morn.

As he sang the chorus of his song, "Oh, dem golden slippers," the men nodded approvingly. When he finished, Primrose said, "Very good, James. You've got talent all right. But let's hear something that all of us know. How about 'Swanee River'?"

Bland hesitated a moment and then said, "Mr. Primrose, I went down to Virginia with my girl, Mannie Friend, a few weeks ago. She was visiting her grandmother who lives down on the White plantation on the peninsula between the James and the York rivers. It was lovely down there, and one afternoon I sat down under a tree by the river bank and picked out a song about Virginia. I'd like to sing a verse of it, if you'll let me."

"All right, son; go ahead," Primrose replied.

That late October afternoon in 1874, James A. Bland, who celebrated his twentieth birthday October 22, began to play and sing his new song. As he sang, the men looked at one another in amazement, captivated by the beauty and simplicity of the new song, for Bland was singing these words:

Carry me back to old Virginny, There's where the cotton and the corn and taters grow;

13

There's where the birds warble sweet in the springtime,
There's where the old darkey's heart am longed to go.

When he finished, Primrose said to Ford, "He's got what Stephen Foster had. That song has everything."

The following Monday night, George Primrose introduced the new song before a packed house in Baltimore and Bland was on his way to fame and fortune. No woman ever won his heart, because music was the one great love of his life. He soon became the outstanding entertainer in the United States, England and even on the continent. He lived abroad for more than twenty years, being lionized wherever he went. But when he came back home to America, the day of the minstrel show was passing. He had been away so long that his name had lost its magic and most of his music had been forgotten. Discouraged and desperate, he returned to Philadelphia, to the scenes of his childhood. And there, at fifty-seven, hungry, penniless and alone, he died of tuberculosis, May 6, 1911. Even the site of his grave in Merion Cemetery, Bala-Cynwyd, near Philadelphia, was quickly forgotten.

Not until thirty years later, on July 15, 1946, was his grave recognized with a stone and his memory recalled with fitting ceremonies. On this occasion the Lions Clubs of Virginia dedicated a monument to his memory and provided money for musical scholarships for worthy Negro students in the state made famous by Bland's finest song. While this homage was belated, it was a genuine and sincere tribute to the man who gave the world, "Oh, dem golden slippers," "In the evening by the moonlight," and the loveliest state song of them all, "Carry me back to old Virginny."

2.

CASEY JONES

Some places are named for people and some people are named for places. When John Luther Jones showed up for work as a fireman with the Mobile and Ohio Railroad in 1882, a brakeman asked, "What's your name, young fellow?" The six-foot-four future engineer replied, "John Luther Jones."

The brakeman continued, "Too bad. We've got three men named John Jones working on this line already. Where are you from?"

"I was born in Missouri in '64, but I call Cayce, Kentucky my home," the youth replied. "Then," said the other man, "your name from now on is going to be Casey Jones." And Casey Jones it became. When the Illinois Central Railroad offered him better wages, he changed jobs and took a room in Mrs. Brady's boarding house, Jackson, Tennessee. It was there he met Janie Brady, who became Mrs. Casey Jones two years later, in 1884. Then, when Casey took over the run from Memphis to Canton, Mississippi, people along the tracks soon learned to recognize the distinctive whistle with which Engineer Jones announced the arrival of Engine 382. When they heard its notes rising on the night air, they said, "There comes Casey Jones."

Casey left his family at Jackson, Tennessee, moved to Memphis and started looking for a new place for his wife and kids. Then came that memorable Sunday, April 29, 1900, a day that was fated to live forever in railroad annals. When Casey came into Memphis from Canton he learned that the engineer slated for the return run had taken sick.

"Casey," he was asked, "could you and Sim double back?"

"I reckon so," the engineer replied. "All right with you, Sim?" His fireman, Sim Webb, nodded his head. "I'll go, Mr. Jones, if you want me to," he said. Casey glanced at his watch. "We're an hour and thirty-five minutes late, Sim. Think we can make it up?" The fireman grinned. "I'll pile on the coal while you open the throttle," he replied. "Then, let her roll," called the engineer. When they passed through Sardis, Casey looked at his watch. "We've made up thirty-five minutes, Sim. Keep shovelling!" At Grenada, Mississippi, he called, "Another twenty-five minutes, Sim. Shovel on the coal and keep her flying!" And when he saw Durant, just thirty-five miles from his destination, he cried, "Just five minutes off schedule, Sim. We'll make it, or die trying!" and he shoved his train into the night with all the steam the boilers could provide. Sim Webb shovelled and sweated and kept pouring on coal as fast as he could.

Casey knew there was a heavy freight in front of him. But Number 83 had orders to pull off and stand by on the siding at Vaughan, Mississippi. Another freight, Number 72, going in the opposite direction, was to join Number 83 on the same siding, since train Number 26, a passenger train, was already sidetracked on the house track above the station at Vaughan. Casey knew the other three trains would be nearby, but he had been assured of a clear track when he went roaring through, enroute to Canton. But when Number 83 pulled off on the side track, her engineer discovered that he could not get all of his cars on the siding, since Number 72 was longer than expected. The engineers consulted each other and agreed that Number 72 would back off the siding on to the main line, so Number 83 could pull all the way off the main line on to the siding at the point where Casey's train would approach Vaughan. Then Casey would stop on the main line between the two freights, while Number 83 backed off on to the main line behind him and Number 72 pulled off the main line on to the siding in front of him. The whole transaction would not take more than five minutes. But when the engineer of Number 72 began to back his train, an air hose burst between the second

16

and third freight cars, nullifying his air brakes and stopping his train, with Number 83 still overlapping the main line with several cars. Three miles away Casey was bearing down on them, unaware of the mixup that had occurred.

Conductor Ed Hoke, of Number 83, had sent Flagman Newberry back up the track to signal Casey that the north switch was clear, but that he was to stop when he got his train by that switch until the south switch was cleared so he could continue his run. But the flagman was already out of sight when the air hose burst. A warning torpedo had been set out, but the other trainmen knew if Casey hit it going at top speed, it would be too late to stop. Casey kept a-coming, and when he hit the torpedo, he reached instinctively to pull back the throttle. But the warning meant "Slow down," not "Stop!"

Through the foggy mist that enshrouded the track, he made out the form of the flagman making wide sawing motions with the lantern in his hand. In another moment he saw the lights on back of the caboose, which, with three other cars, still overlapped the main line from Number 83. Then it was too late. Sim saw it too, and shouted, "Goin' to hit, Mr. Jones. Better jump." But Casey pulled the throttle back with all his might, set the emergency brakes and grabbed the whistle cord, while Sim leaped out of the cab into the night. Despite his frantic efforts, Casey's train tore into the wooden caboose of Number 83, and splintered its way through the next two boxcars, scattering cargo far and wide. Back up the track, Sim Webb staggered to his feet, dazed and bruised, but alive. But in the cab of Engine 382, the whistle cord still clutched in his hand, lay Casey Jones, the only fatality, dead of a broken neck. Jim Gaffney, engineer of passenger train Number 26, telegraphed the news to the world.

It was an insignificant wreck as train wrecks go. The engine was salvaged and rebuilt and served her masters for nearly thirty years longer. But the men up and down the lines who knew, admired and respected Casey Jones couldn't get him out of their minds. One friend especially, a cinder-pit man, Wallace

Saunders, and his helper, Ike Wentworth, continued to grieve over Casey's accidental death. Soon the roundhousemen up and down the line began to hear of a song which the two men had written, a sort of sentimental railroad ballad extolling the virtues of the late lamented engineer and honoring him after his tragic death. Later on, two professional song-writers polished up the verses, changed the locale of the accident, added some stanzas of their own and gave to the world the railroader's favorite, "Casey Jones."

These pioneers of the iron rails say that to this day in some sections of Tennessee and Mississippi, on foggy nights when everything is dark and still, the long low moan of a train whistle can be heard far in the distance, rising to a screaming crescendo, and then dying away in the night. When that happens, the old-timers say to each other, "It's Casey Jones, riding through the night, back to his grave in Jackson, Tennessee."

3.

DARLING NELLIE GRAY

"It was awful, Benjamin. I swear it was the vilest thing I've ever seen." The young man shook his head as if to erase the memory from his mind. "The auctioneer stood there and shouted 'What am I offered for this black man?' and 'Make me an offer for this black wench. She'll do the work of two during the day and— Well, somebody make me an offer!' "

"And they sold them like cattle," added the other student. "Just like a bunch of cattle. And everyone is a human being, not an animal."

"Those auctioneers acted more like animals than the people they were selling," the first youth said. "Something's got to be done to stop it. It's wrong; it's sinful. That's what it is—sinful."

His friend interrupted, "What about those pious sermons we've been reading defending slavery from the Bible."

"You can defend any vice or declare any virtue from the Bible. Those sermons about slavery are based entirely on the Old Testament. It's Jesus who made the difference, not Abraham or Moses or David and Solomon," the other suggested. "But bad or good it's going on right under our noses and we're powerless to do anything about it," he continued. "What about it, Benjamin? What can college students do about this vile and evil thing?"

Benjamin Russell Hanby didn't answer his college mate immediately. After a few moments of serious thought he replied, "I'm afraid it's gone beyond us. I'm afraid it has gotten too big for any man or group or even any state to cope with. It can only end one way."

"What way? War?" the others asked, almost in unison. Hanby nodded his head. "Both sides have gone too far to back down now. This is 1856. War may come in one year or five years or ten years, but I don't see any other way out, short of a miracle."

"It would be a righteous war, if there ever was one," the first young man continued. "After seeing that slave auction today, I'd feel perfectly justified in taking up arms to destroy slavery once and for all."

"I only wish it were that easy," Hanby said. "But wars never solve problems; they always create more problems."

"Have you seen a slave auction?" his college chum asked.

"Yes," Hanby replied. "And I've known of worse evils."

"What, for instance?"

"A slave auction that divided a happy family."

"When was that?" his friends asked.

"Years ago, when I was a small boy," the twenty-three-year-old Otterbein College student continued, "a fugitive slave stopped at our home late one night. He had been running for hours and was completely exhausted."

"What did your father do, Benjamin?"

"He did what you and I would have done. He took him in, washed him, clothed him, fed him, and gave him a safe spot to sleep in for a few hours before resuming his flight to freedom."

"Did they catch him?"

"No," Benjamin added, "but the tragedy of it all was that he never knew what had happened to his wife."

"She wasn't with him?" one of the students asked.

"No," Hanby replied. "He told us that she had been sold to a plantation owner down in Georgia for $750.00. And he kept repeating her name over and over again, 'Nellie Gray, Nellie Gray.' I can almost close my eyes and hear him talking as he tossed in his sleep, 'I'll come and get you, Nellie Gray, and nobody will take you from me any more.' He said that several times during the night. The next morning we gave him some food and a little money and sent him on his way. From Ken-

20

tucky to Ohio and on to Canada. What a life! What a horrible, dreadful life for a human being!"

"Did he make it?"

"We never knew. But father turned to me after the runaway had gone and said, 'Benjamin, since you are planning to study theology and prepare yourself for the Christian ministry, don't ever forget what you have seen and heard this day, and do what you can to see that it never happens again.' So I ask myself as I ask you—What can a college sophomore do to stop this insanity!"

The conversation broke up about midnight, and the students retired to their various rooms, crammed a few lessons for the next day's classes and prepared for bed. Westerville, Ohio, where Otterbein College was located, is a typical, sleepy little college town. But there was little sleep for Benjamin Hanby that fateful night in 1856. He tossed back and forth on his bed as rest was denied him, and as thoughts of the evening's "bull session" continued to haunt his sleepless hours. In a semi-dream, he thought he saw the fugitive slave of his childhood sitting near a low green valley in old Kentucky; a moment later the black man was singing a mournful song about his sweetheart who had been taken away. Then he saw him sitting by the river, weeping in his agony. When he could stand it no longer, Hanby threw back the covers and leaped to his feet, shouting, "He's a human being, too, with feelings, and they treat him like a beast." He paced the floor as the words of a poem began to fashion themselves in his mind. Picking up his banjo, he sat on the side of the bed, picked out a few random chords, and began to write a new song. He started with these lines:

There's a low green valley on the old Kentucky shore
Where I've whiled many happy hours away;
A-sitting and a-singing by the little cottage door,
Where lived my darling Nellie Gray.
Oh, my poor Nellie Gray, They have taken you away,
And I'll never see my darling any more.
I'm sitting by the river and I'm weeping all the day
For you've gone from the old Kentucky shore.

21

A few days later he wrote out the words and music of his new song. Encouraged by his college chums and classmates, he mailed a copy to a music publisher in Boston. The publisher knew a good thing when he heard it and promptly printed it and offered copies for sale. Strangely enough, the author didn't even know that his song had been accepted until he saw a copy in a music store in Columbus, Ohio, the following year. When he wrote to the firm in Boston, they very politely notified him that since he had overlooked copyrighting the song in his own name, they had done it in their name. The publisher added, " 'Nellie Gray' is sung on both sides of the Atlantic. We have made the money and you the fame. That balances the account."

"He should have sued them," a friend remarked when he learned what had happened. "He did," another explained. "And his lawyer settled out of court for $100 and kept $50 of that as his fee."

Hanby, whose "Nellie Gray" became as famous as the novel, "Uncle Tom's Cabin," shares whatever glory there may be in arousing sentiments which culminated in the tragic War Between the States. But he made up for it by dashing off a simple little Christmas song for some children he knew. Strangely enough, this ditty continues to be sung to this day. It is the perennial favorite of children the world over, "Up on the Housetop."

Hanby died at thirty-four, in Westerville, Ohio, March 16, 1867, having seen the war his song helped start fought to a victorious finish, and the evil of slavery which he hated with all his heart forever banished from American soil.

NOTE: Benjamin Hanby was the son of William Hanby, who was at various times the editor of "The Religious Telescope," publishing agent and later Bishop of the United Brethren Church. The house in which "Nellie Gray" was written is still preserved as the Hanby Historic House Museum at Westerville, Ohio.

4.

DIXIE

Sunday morning, September 18, 1859, was a rainy, dismal morning in New York City. Daniel Decatur Emmett, a singer with the famous Bryant's Minstrels, and his wife, were cooped up in a cheap boarding house room on Catherine Street. "I can stand a blue Monday," Dan said to his wife, "but a blue Sunday, well, that's another matter." He rose, walked slowly to the window, looked out on the rain-swept streets and sighed. "Boy, what a day! And on our one day off in the week."

Mrs. Emmett shared his feelings, "It would happen like this, Dan, wouldn't it?"

"Yes, dear," he answered, "but it can't last forever. There's just so much water up there and when it all falls down, there's none left." She joined him at the window. "Now take last Sunday," she said. "Wasn't it a perfectly lovely day? Warm and sunny and a day that made you glad to be alive."

Dan shrugged his shoulders. "But on a day like this," the forty-four-year-old entertainer said, "I'd swap New York City for a spot in Dixie, even if New York is the biggest city in the land." "So would I," Mrs. Emmett added.

Dixie—a magic word, conjuring up scenes of lazy living along the Mississippi, or Colonels and their lovely ladies sipping juleps in the blue-grass region of Kentucky. Dixie—darkies chopping cotton near Charleston or lifting huge bales on to the barges at Memphis or chanting their mournful spirituals in the cool of the evening outside their cabin doors back of the huge mansions that graced many a spacious plantation in those ante-bellum days.

Dan looked at his wife. "I was fifteen when I wrote 'Old Dan

Tucker,' and I haven't written a successful song since. Do you think I'm all washed up, honey?"

"No, darling. Your day will come. Just be patient," she pleaded. "Maybe when we get back to Dixie you'll get the break you deserve."

Dixie. Some folks said that the word was a corruption of the name of the surveyor Dixon, who, with Mason, surveyed that famous line that became a symbolic line of demarcation between the north and the south. Others claimed it originated in New Orleans, where the French population used the word "dix" for a piece of paper money. The rich folks who had a lot of "dix-es" were jokingly called "Dixies." But others remembered a land owner named Mr. Dixie who once had large holdings on Manhattan Island. When New York state was about to pass a bill outlawing slavery after 1822, he shipped his slaves south and sold them to the southern plantation owners. Whoever bought Mr. Dixie's slaves didn't treat them like he had, so they would say one to another, "If we could only get back to Mr. Dixie's, everything would be all right." Soon the word was passing from one plantation to another and from one state to another. Then someone dropped the " 's" after the name and the "Mr." before it, leaving just the word "Dixie." But it symbolized freedom for the oppressed and liberty for the downtrodden. The overseers ridiculed the new word, however, but they could not prevent the darkies from speaking of it, first in hushed tones and then openly. Soon the white people picked it up, applying the word to that section of the country lying south of the Mason-Dixon line and east of the Mississippi River.

Dan and Jerry Bryant, joint owners of "Bryant's Minstrels," knocked on Dan Emmett's door that rainy afternoon with a strange request. "Dan Emmett," Jerry Bryant said, after they had been admitted to the room, "Dan and I think the show needs some pepping-up."

"I agree, Jerry," the Ohio-born entertainer replied. "But what's that got to do with me?"

"Just this," Dan Bryant said. "Jerry and I want you to write

24

a new song, a new walk-around. We think that's just what the show needs."

"And when do you want the new song?" Emmett asked.

Jerry Bryant scratched his head. "We don't want to rush you, Dan, but how about tomorrow night?"

"How about what tomorrow night, Jerry?" asked Emmett.

"The song, Dan; the new song," the co-owner replied.

"You mean you want the new song for Monday night's show?" inquired the composer. "Why not?" asked the Bryant brothers jointly. "Why wait a week when the show needs a shot in the arm right away?"

Dan Emmett looked over at his wife. "What about it, honey?"

"You can do it, Dan. You've got it in you. All you have to do is to get it out of you," she answered.

"What theme?" he continued, addressing the question to his wife.

"Dixie," she said. "All right," he said, "I'll do what I can."

"We knew you'd come through, Dan," said Jerry Bryant. "You always have." And Jerry and Dan Bryant quickly left the room, leaving Dan Emmett and his wife alone.

"Here is your chance," she told him. "Take all your dreams about Dixie, the cotton fields, buckwheat cakes and cornmeal batter, a side of bacon and a darkie's dream of heaven; tie them all up in a big knot, shake them together, and then let the music roll out like only a good minstrel man can. And I'll see you at supper." She closed the door behind her as she quietly slipped out of the room.

Dan Emmett began to work on different phrases, trying to find the right meter and mood for his new song. First he began with, "Diss worl' was made in jiss six days and finished up in various ways, Hoorah—hoorah—" but soon discarded that and began again with these lines: "I wish I was in the land of cotton, Ole times dar am not forgotten, Look away, Look away, Look away, Dixie land." Finishing the first verse with three more lines in the same meter and spirit, he hammered out a chorus that was a minstrel man's dream: "Den I wish I was in Dixie, Hooray,

25

Hooray! In Dixie land I'll take my stand to lib and die in Dixie. Away, away, away down south in Dixie!"

Introduced by the composer at Mechanic's Hall the very next night, Monday, September 19, 1859, it became immediately popular. The south quickly adopted it as an official song, though written by a northern man in a northern city about a northerner. Unfortunately, the composer was later criticized and upbraided in his native north for supposed disloyalty to the Union, and, until the Civil War ended, he had a hard time making a living. He finally retired to a small farm at his birthplace, Mount Vernon, Ohio, where he and his family lived in seclusion for many years. Although he was once almost lynched in New York because the Yankees considered him a southern spy, due to his song "Dixie," he lived to see his "walk-around" win universal acclaim. Later he said, "If I'd known it was going to be so popular, I'd have written it better."

His declining years were made more comfortable by the recognition due him as an entertainer and song-writer. He died at Mount Vernon, Ohio, June 28, 1904, in his eighty-eighth year, the only Yankee whose casket was lowered into the ground to the strains of a Confederate song, "Dixie."

5.

DOWN BY THE OLD MILL STREAM

"Down by the old mill stream," despite the sentimentality that oozes from every bar of the music, is the story of a song-writer who lost a fortune, and a girl who became a notorious criminal.

The girl was angel-faced Buda Goodman, the daughter of a race sheet writer, who was born in Chicago in 1888. Her father said of her, "Buda has a high spirit and a gentle way that makes her even less predictable than horses." But she had a "poignant beauty and quick understanding," so her father sent her to a finishing school, St. Joseph's Academy, in Adrian, Michigan. But she didn't grow into the young woman he expected; she had too much of his blood in her veins, and when she returned home she began to associate with the racing and gambling crowd, much to his distress.

The composer, Tell Taylor, was an Ohio boy who grew up along the Blanchard River near Findlay. When he grew into young manhood he tried his hand at teaching school at the old Robinson red brick schoolhouse near his home, but soon left the security of a desk, blackboard and a room full of noisy kids, for the uncertain life of an oil-field roustabout. That must have proved too hectic, because the next job he found was that of a shoe-clerk. But music was in his bones and would not be denied.

In 1906, by some strange quirk of fate, Tell met Buda and fell in love with her. During their courting days, the two lovers used to walk hand-in-hand down to an old grist mill near Findlay, known around those parts as Misamore Mill. And it was there that Tell was inspired to write his most famous song for the girl of his dreams. But the dreams soon turned into nightmares, and they were divorced after only four years of marriage. Tell Taylor said, "I married Buda when we both were drunk and I found out she was quite incapable of loyalty to anybody." Buda was too beautiful and too much of a schemer to care what anyone thought of her or said about her. The Police, however, soon dubbed her "The Queen of the Badger Game." A group of gangsters, using beautiful Buda as bait, laid traps for rich, unwary business men, and the extortionists soon were reputed to be "a million dollar outfit." Detective Dannenberg set the countertrap that finally snared her, and the Supreme Court was compelled to rewrite The Mann Act in order to save innocent suckers from falling prey to her kind. Buda spent her later years in a comfortable New York City apartment, where, it was rumored, gamblers and gangsters were welcome guests. Convicted of being involved in a jewelry robbery, she served several years in Auburn prison, and then vanished from sight.

Tell Taylor didn't have to steal for a living, but, for some years the pickings from writing music were mighty thin. He plugged his songs in music stores and silent movie houses during the week and in the sheet music departments of Findlay's larger business houses on Saturdays. A brief stage career saw his name on the same billing with such notables as Sophie Tucker, Weber and Fields and Al Jolson. From Chicago he went to New York, opening up a music publishing house there with Jimmy Walker, future Mayor, and composer Ernest Ball. But that did not do the business the three song-writers and their financial backer expected, so it soon closed. Back to Chicago went the erstwhile actor, playing parts in several successful productions before opening up his own publishing house in that mid-western metropolis. It was there that fame and fortune finally caught up with him.

A well-known male quartet known as "The Orpheus Comedy Four" paid him a visit in his new establishment one afternoon. "We want a new song, Tell," one of the men said. "What do you have?"

Since Berlin's "Alexander's Rag Time Band" was all the rage

at the time, Tell decided that a slow sentimental ballad would be just the thing. "The public likes rag time one year and smooth harmonious numbers the next," he explained. "And this is the time to counteract the beat of Berlin with something slow and easy." He gave them the manuscript of "Down by the old mill stream," little dreaming that the girl who had inspired it was almost in the clutches of the law at that very moment. The quartet sang it, and the song became a hit overnight. Money began pouring in, as much as $1,000 a month when it was at the height of its popularity. When he thought he had exhausted its financial possibilities, Tell Taylor sold the copyright for some $60,000. At that, it was almost worth having an unfortunate love affair; very few of them pay off so handsomely. The money went out almost as rapidly as it came in, and before long, he found his funds depleted. Too many so-called friends had sponged on him for too much over too long a period of time. So he sold his Chicago publishing house and moved back home to Findlay, Ohio, in 1920, hoping to recoup his fortune, and spending his last years on a farm he had purchased for his parents years before. His greatest ambition was to live long enough to produce a motion picture based on the title of his finest song. When he died, November 23, 1937, he was in Chicago making final arrangements for the scenario of the new movie.

At that he fared better than Nat Ayer. This American-born composer made several fortunes, but was plagued with misfortune almost as much as he was blessed with fortune itself. He went broke three times, despite the fact that he had made over $12,000 in royalties from "If you were the only girl in the world" and close to $50,000 from "Oh, you beautiful doll." When he went bankrupt in 1938 he listed his assets as 'None' and his liabilities as $6,652.00. Illness, accidents and bad investments plagued him, but he won a discharge from bankruptcy ten years later when he finally paid his last bill. Each time he went busted he would say to his friends, "This is where I start all over again." He suffered a broken finger during a V-2 rocket raid in England during the second world war, but he was still able to play his tunes on the piano until his death at sixty-five in 1952, in Bath, England. Appropriately he collapsed while walking in the Abbey Churchyard.

Not as fortunate, however, was Maude Nugent. In 1901 she signed away all rights for her new song, "Sweet Rosie O'Grady", for $200. In 1946 she sued Twentieth-Century Fox Motion Picture Company for $12,500,000, charging that they had unlawfully used the title of her song as the title of a movie. A Manhattan judge disagreed and threw her case out of court!

6.

FOR HE'S A JOLLY GOOD FELLOW

The gospel song, "Safe in the arms of Jesus," although written for and first introduced at a large Sunday School rally, has now been almost completely taken over by the morticians and funeral directors. Its joyous notes now mingle with the sad and dolorous cadences of the death march. Just the opposite is the history of the rousing song of conviviality, "For he's a jolly good fellow." It began at a funeral and ended up in a tavern.

When the knights of old sallied forth from their castles to wrest the Holy Land from pagan hands, and began the movements described in history books as The Crusades, many of them never came back alive. One lady climbed often to the castle tower, looking off into the distance for some sign of her beloved's return. When day after day passed and no whirl of dust beneath a horse's hoofs and no distant beating of victorious drums heralded his coming, she cried out in the words of the mother of Sisera, after he had been slain with a tent pin by Jael in ancient Israel, "Why is his chariot so long in coming? Why tarry the wheels of his chariots? Have they not sped? Have they not divided the spoils?"

Then it was that she caught a glimpse of her knight's page, but, to her horror, the lad was clothed in black, the color of death. She cried out, "What news do you bring, my bonnie page? He was to have returned by Easter and, lo, Easter is past and Trinity is past and he has not come!"

The page replied, "My lady, the news I bring will cause you to weep. So take off your gold and your silver and put away your jewels in their casket. For my lord has been slain in battle fighting the infidel, and now his body lies buried under other skies than ours. I saw four of his fellow knights bearing his body to its final resting place. One carried his curiass, one his shield, one his sword and the other bore nothing but an aching heart as he walked beside his coffin. Over his grave they scattered what flowers they could gather and what garlands their gnarled hands could fashion, and over him the nightingale sang, chanting his final requiem. We sang of his victories and boasted of his prowess with the sword, and then left him alone with his glory."

Out of the agony of a thousand similar scenes came the moving strains of a funeral dirge in which the heart-broken loved ones sang of the departed dead and of the majesty that crowned their closing hours. "My knight has gone to battle, but when will he return?" they sang, and the song spread rapidly from widow to widow, and from fatherless child to fatherless child, and from castle to castle, spanning rivers and continents and binding together the vast army of the bereaved. "Oh, when will he return?" they asked. "Oh, when will he return?" they sang, to the slow measures of the first versions of what is today an entirely different kind of a song for an entirely different kind of a mood.

But how could such a song go from pathos to buffoonery? By what steps did it take its downward march? In the year 1566 some unknown minstrel sang a lament on the death of the Duke of Guise, which resembled the older song, that dated as far back as the twelfth and thirteenth centuries. The melody was then revived after having been almost forgoten for generations. Then, on the night of September 11, 1709, in the camp of the Marshal de Villars, at Quesnoy, a few miles from the scene of the battle of Malplaquet, someone else took up the familiar strains, using the tune for a song which ridiculed and heaped scorn upon the enemy, embodied in a man by the name of Marlborough, Marbrough or Malbrook. The song that originated centuries earlier now became, instead of a solemn lament, a rather ridiculous burlesque, commemorating the fortunes and misfortunes of war.

When Marie Antoinette heard Madame Potrine sing the tune as a lullably for the infant Dauphin, she began singing it herself, and soon the song became a part of the gay life of the cafes and courtyards of pre-revolutionary France. Even Napoleon knew the tune; he is said to have hummed it as his vast armies crossed the Neimen River at the outset of the tragic Russian invasion of 1812. "Malbrook has gone to war," they sang, "But when will he return?" "He won't come home until morning, He won't come home until morning, He won't come home until morning, Till daylight doth appear," they replied.

Whether the words referred to the English Duke of Marlborough, whom the French hated with a holy passion, or whether he just happened to come along in time to be the butt of their jests, has never been accurately determined. But the tune was too good to forget, so the British quickly picked it up, just like the Yankees had taken over from the English the song 'Yankee Doodle' which had been written to ridicule them by their allies in the French and Indian War in America in 1755. But instead of singing it to herald the news of a fighting man's death on the battlefield, they used it to give the soldiers a rousing send-off when they left home. "For he's a jolly good fellow, Which no one can deny," they sang enthusiastically, little dreaming that they were appropriating a funeral dirge for their farewell song. And by the time the song had leaped the Atlantic, the Americans went even further than their British cousins and began to sing, as they staggered home from an evening of over-indulgence at the neighbourhood saloon, "We won't be home until morning, We'll be lucky to get there at all," which was literally true!

While there are today many conflicting stories about the origin of the music, no one can deny that what had been created as a lament for the honored dead has now degenerated into a "serenade of the sickening soaks."

7.

HAPPY BIRTHDAY TO YOU

"Miss Patty," one of the little girls said, "that little boy over there said that this place was a kinney-garden. And I told him that your name wasn't Miss Kinney but Miss Patty, and that this was a Patty-garden."

Miss Patty Smith Hill smiled. "It happens that both of you are mistaken," she replied. "It is neither a kinney-garden nor a Patty-garden. Does any child know what this really is?"

A young boy held up his hand. "I know, Miss Patty. It's a kinner-garden, because the other teachers, Miss Mildred and Miss Jessica, are kin to you." The three sisters laughed merrily, and Miss Mildred said, "That's the most original one yet." But Miss Jessica said, "No, it isn't, Mildred. I think I can beat that. One of my star pupils told me that he wondered why this school was called a kidney-garden, because kidneys don't grow in gardens; they grow in people." Miss Mildred held up her hands. "I surrender. You win. But we'd better straighten the children out or they will be so confused they'll never know the truth."

Miss Patty then explained that the word was really 'kindergarten' and that it came from two German words which meant 'a garden of children.' "If it's a garden," one lad interrupted, "then there are too many weeds in here to suit me." Miss Jessica struggled to choke back a laugh, and said, "Maybe the others are the flowers and you are the weed. Did you ever think about that?" The boy shook his head and said no more. Miss Patty continued, "Now, I'm going to ask you a question and I want you to give me the answer all together. Ready?" "Ready," the children replied, almost in unison. "All right. Here is my question. What is a kindergarten?" their teacher asked. The children answered enthusiastically, "A garden of children." "Correct," their teacher said. "Now whenever anyone asks you where you go every morning, you tell them you go to the kindergarten where Miss Patty Hill and here two sisters teach the little boys and girls of Louisville, Kentucky who are too young to go to school. Now let's sing." The children gathered about her when she took her place at the piano and the next fifteen minutes were spent in singing all kinds of songs about all kinds of things that make up the delightful world of little boys and girls.

Some years earlier, the three talented daughters of the distinguished Presbyterian minister, educator, editor and college president, Dr. William Wallace Hill, had organized the Louisville Kindergarten Training School, to help develop and popularize the kindergarten movement in the United States. At the request of the children, and because she could find no suitable songs for kindergarten use, Miss Patty began to improvise melodies and write verses on a wide variety of subjects to suit almost every occasion. Soon her pupils were looking forward to "singing time" as much as to any other phase of the day's program. One morning in 1893 she said to her two sisters, "We need some little song with which to begin the day's program."

"What about a hymn?" suggested Mildred.

"That's not what I had in mind," Patty explained. "I want something very simple, so simple that the youngest child could pick it up in a moment."

Jessica interrupted, "The first thing we say to each other every morning is 'Good Morning.' Why not write a 'Good Morning' song or something like that, beginning with 'Good morning children?"

Patty was pleased. "Make it just 'Good morning to you' and you'll have exactly what I want.

"The children could sing to us, 'Good morning dear teacher' and we could reply to them, 'Good morning dear children,' " added Mildred.

"Perfect," said Patty. Turning to the piano she struck a chord in the key of G and in a few minutes picked out a very simple tune for an equally simple verse that began with the words 'Good morning to you.' The next day the teachers sang their lines for the children and the children sang their words for the teachers. And from that day, the singing of the new song became the first order of the day for the Louisville kindergarten. Miss Patty, smart enough to know a good thing when she stumbled across it, had the presence of mind to make a copy of her new song and copyright it with the copyright division of the Library of Congress. Not that she expected to make a fortune out of it, but just to protect her interests and that of her sisters as the author-composer. It wasn't until a few months later that one of her pupils came up with an equally thrilling brainstorm.

Just after the opening exercises, and the usual singing of "Good morning to you," one of the little girls spoke up and said, "Miss Patty, yesterday was my birthday."

"Did you have a party?" her teacher inquired.

"Oh, yes," she replied. "And we played games and put on party hats and had all the ice cream and cake we could eat. And do you know what?"

"What?" Miss Patty asked.

"The children who came to my party sang a happy birthday song to me."

"A happy birthday song," her teacher asked. "Where did you get it?"

"Oh," continued the little lass, "I wrote it for them. I just took your song 'Good morning to you' and changed it to 'Happy Birthday to you' and had the children sing it for me at my party."

Patty glanced over at Mildred, who was already staring at Jessica. "That seems to take care of that," Jessica said. "Now we will have to recognize every birthday with a 'Happy Birthday' song." And strangely enough, the Happy Birthday song caught on more rapidly than had the original 'Good morning' song. In fact, it caught on so well that soon people were playing and singing it in public as well as in private without the slightest idea that the music had been copyrighted by the Kentucky kindergarten teacher years before.

Miss Patty joined the faculty of Teachers' College, Columbia University, in 1910 as the director of the kindergarten department. She was in great demand as a lecturer and travelled widely speaking on the subject that was dearest to her heart. She and her sisters published "Song Stories for Kindergarten," and dedicated it "Respectfully to the Louisville Free Kindergarten Association." In 1935, as Dr. Patty Smith Hill, she retired as professor emeritus of education at Columbia, and died in New York City eleven years later, at the age of seventy-eight. Her body was brought to Louisville, and there, on May 30, 1946, she was buried in beautiful Cave Hill Cemetery.

Just as childless Mrs. Effie Carlton wrote 'Rock-a-bye Baby' for other mothers to sing to their little babies, so Dr. Patty Hill, who never married, wrote the most delightful song with which grandparents, parents, brothers and sisters, uncles and aunts, and all other relatives celebrate each other's birthdays within the joyous intimacy of the family circle.

8.

HOME ON THE RANGE

The buffalo used to roam the plains of Kansas in wild profusion until "Buffalo Bill" Cody came on the scene. They say that during the 1860s he personally killed 4,280 buffalo within eighteen months, selling the meat to railroad workers' camps and the commissary of Fort Hays nearby. Anyway, they don't play there like they used to. And about the only place you'll find one today is in a government preserve, or on an old nickel or in the song "Home on the range" which begins "O give me a home where the buffalo roam."

When the city of Hutchinson, Kansas was laid off in November 1871, the streets were marked with buffalo bones. By the end of 1875, buffalo herds that used to number in excess of twenty-five million had been practically exterminated; at one time their bones were used as legal tender in Dodge City. The Daltons picked up where the animals left off, and roamed the prairies almost at will, robbing and shooting with unrestrained violence until they were slain at Coffeyville in 1892.

But the glory of Kansas didn't die with the buffalo or the Daltons. She can boast that the most popular song written nearest the geographical center of the United States was composed within her borders. Back in the 1870s, life was lonesome out on the plains. The ranchers and cowhands and homesteaders lived so far apart that they seldom saw each other. The only time neighbours got together was in Church or at a funeral or in the over-crowded main street of the nearest frontier town on a rousing Saturday night. And "home" was either a palatial mansion in one of the big cities back east, or a covered wagon moving west, or a tiny, weatherbeaten shack somewhere along the way. It was anywhere you hung up your hat on the way to fame and fortune.

As for culture, it was limited to the intelligence of the nearest preacher, or the drunken judge who tried to dispense law and justice, even if he had to back up his decisions with a six-shooter, or one of those few and far between school teachers who were hired to teach the kids of the wealthy how to read and write. The guitar and banjo provided what musical accompaniments there were when the cowboys gathered around a fire late at night, or when the folks wanted to sing a hymn of a Sunday morning. If you couldn't play a fiddle, you knew someone who could; and if you could, you were in constant demand.

One of these homesteaders, Dr. Brewster Higley, stepped through the front door of his rickety cabin one morning in 1873. Looking out over East Beaver Creek, he said to himself, "Home—and what a home." He gazed out over the expanse of prairie and, in his mind's eye, saw the herds of buffalo go thundering by, leaving great clouds of dust in their wake. "Soon there won't be one within a thousand miles," he said. "And then they'll be shooting down the deer and after that, the antelope, and there'll be nothing left but land stretching out as far as the eye can see. And the range will be as silent as a tomb, and as devoid of life as an empty grave."

Dan Kelley lived twenty miles away, in a little place called "Gaylord," a trading post in Smith County. He was well-known throughout that part of the state because he was an excellent guitar player. Dr. Higley knew Dan as a friend as well as a musician, and often told him, "If I ever write a poem, I'm going to get you to set it to music."

"I'll do it, Doc. Just let me know when you're ready."

Well, that morning in 1873, Dr. Higley felt ready. There was a song inside of him that was just crying to be sung. It was a song about the range and the life that used to roam the plains before the days of the greedy, fast-shooting white man; and the home that could be built there and the "desert that could be made to blossom like the rose" and the "mirage that could become a pool." Soon he was saying these words to himself:

O give me a home where the buffalo roam, Where the deer and the antelope play;
Where seldom is heard a discouraging word And the skies are not cloudy all day.

For the chorus, he took a cue from the successful and popular Negro spirituals, and merely repeated the lines of the verse, with little change in words or music:

Home, home on the range, Where the deer and the antelope play,
Where seldom is heard a discouraging word And the skies are not cloudy all day.

There were other verses about the wild curlew's scream, and even a vision of a "graceful white swan" that went "gliding along, like a maid in a heavenly dream," about as impossible as a dream could be. But he worked it into his stanzas, and when he saw Dan Kelley a few weeks later, he gave him a copy of the words and a hint as to the music he hoped his friend would compose. Dan did himself noble with the music, and, between the two lonely Kansas homesteaders, "Home on the range" was born. While some people later on suggested that the meter and music were borrowed from the familiar hymn, "Home of the soul," it isn't any more likely than that the Hawaiian national song "Aloha" was a "steal" from the gospel song "Pass me not, O gentle Saviour," despite their evident similarities.

After it became universally popular, everyone tried to take credit for it and to cash in on its success. In fact, some folks in Arizona entered a suit for half a million dollars in 1934, claiming that the song was their property, and that they were due the money for "alleged infringement of their copyright." But the truth is that the author never bothered to copyright the song at all, and it had long since passed into public domain.

When a resourceful New York lawyer dug up the facts, everyone who sang or sold "Home on the range" breathed a sigh of relief.

Franklin D. Roosevelt told the country that this was his favorite, so it was played in his honor as President of the United States, times without number, and was as popular the day he died as the morning he took the oath of office. And today, in crowded cities, where "range" means the kitchen stove, instead of the wide open spaces, drug-store cowboys join with their mid-western and far-western comrades in singing their number one song, "Home on the range." Many of those who sing it out in the open, long to exchange the range for the crowded city streets, while many who sing it in the cities wouldn't know what to do with themselves if they were suddenly stranded "out in the middle of no-where," way out west in Kansas!

9.

HOME SWEET HOME

Even though Mr. W. W. Corcoran was eighty-four he didn't want to miss the parade. The people of Washington, D.C. were turning out en masse to welcome Lieut. George Melville and his band of Arctic explorers home by giving a mammoth parade in their honor. That October afternoon in 1882 was a memorable one, because, when the bands marched by playing "Home Sweet Home," the aged philanthropist recalled that the author of that famous poem had been denied a home as much in life as in death.

"I remember seeing Payne play 'Hamlet' and 'Romeo' when he was a lad of only seventeen, and when I had to pay $50 for a seat," Mr. Corcoran remarked to a friend. "But he was a credit to the American stage. And now, thirty years following his death in Tunis, North Africa, his remains are still buried far from the soil of his native land and thousands of miles from the country which he immortalized in his famous poem."

"What can be done about it?" the friend asked.

"I'm not sure," the older man replied, "but I'm going to ask our Secretary of State to communicate with our ambassador in London, to see if he can arrange with Earl Granville to secure permission from the Tunisian authorities to let me bring Payne's body home to the United States."

"Quite complicated, isn't it?"

"Maybe, but we owe it to Payne for writing 'Home Sweet Home,' and I'll bear the entire expense of the undertaking myself," Mr. Corcoran continued. And he was right. Years had passed since that evening in Paris in 1822 when thirty-

42

year-old John Howard Payne had looked out over the rooftops of the city, longing for a glimpse of an old house in Easthampton, Long Island, where he had spent several happy boyhood years. To his laurels as an actor he had added further garlands as a playwright, and he was in France seeking such theatrical successes as could be readily adapted for his English employers. Sir Henry Bishop had written a simple tune adapted from a Sicilian air for a poem, "To the home of my childhood in sorrow I came," for a forthcoming opera, "Clari, or The Maid of Milan." But Payne was not satisfied with the words or the mood of the stanzas. That night in Paris, gripped by homesickness such as he had never experienced before, he wrote the five stanzas of his immortal hymn, to be sung to the music already composed by the famous musician. One night in May, 1823, seven months later, Miss Maria Tree introduced the song when "Clari" opened in London's Covent Garden. Needless to say, it was an instantaneous success. It was introduced in the United States on Thursday, November 12, when the opera opened in New York City that same fall. Payne sold his copyright for $250 and the publishers realized more than $10,000 from the song.

From that day on, everything Payne touched seemed to crumble into dust. He worked for several years among the American Indians, particularly the Cherokees, championing their cause and arguing on their behalf before government authorities. For his zeal he suffered a term of imprisonment in 1835 in a cabin not far from Dalton, Georgia. Then he turned again to writing, but the magic touch that had created his popular tragedy "Brutus" years before had left him; the creative flame had dwindled to a mere spark, which had sputtered and then gone out. Daniel Webster and other friends came to his rescue, and, in 1842, they persuaded President John Tyler to appoint Payne U.S. Consul to the Kingdom of Tunis, North Africa. There, after two terms as Consul, and following a long and lingering illness, he died at the age of sixty, April 9, 1852. After fitting ceremonies, attended by a few pall-bearers and several close friends, he was buried in the Protestant Cemetery of St.

George, where his body was to lie unmolested for more than a quarter of a century.

Many years earlier he had fallen in love with Mary Shelley, the widow of the famous English poet. But he felt she was more interested in his literary friend, Washington Irving, than in him. She married neither, and Payne remained a bachelor the rest of his days. The house which his friends built for him in Washington was never occupied by the famous poet, who had taken up residence in a "house not made with hands" before returning to his homeland to receive this gift from the hands of his admirers.

But Mr. Corcoran got to work immediately, and letters fairly flew across the Atlantic and the Mediterranean, until, with the full consent of all governments involved, the body of John Howard Payne was exhumed in Tunis on January 5, 1883. The remains were placed reverently in a new coffin which was sealed inside a strong iron-bound box and addressed to U.S. Consul Fish, Marseilles, France. The "Burgundia" picked up the coffin there and deposited it in New York City on March 22, 1883. Funeral services were scheduled to be held on the ninety-first anniversary of the poet's birth, June 9, at Oak Hill Cemetery, Georgetown, just outside the city of Washington, D.C. to be attended by President Chester A. Arthur, Cabinet members, Representatives from both houses of Congress as well as members of the diplomatic corps.

The procession left the Corcoran Art Gallery in Washington at 4 P.M., arriving at the cemetery at 5:15 P.M., the aged philanthropist, despite his advanced years, taking part in the activities of the afternoon. The President of Columbia University, Dr. J. C. Welling, acted as chairman of the committee on arrangements, while Rev. W. A. Leonard and Rev. Dr. Pinkney were the officiating clergymen. Robert S. Chilton, poet of the day, read some original verses honoring the exile's return, after which a distinguished member of the Washington Bar, Leigh Robinson, delivered the principal address. Following the interment, the Philharmonic Society, directed by Professor Wid-

dows, with the full Marine Band, sang "The Hallelujah Chorus" from "The Messiah." Bishop Pinkney then pronounced the benediction, after which the Band played "Safe in the Arms of Jesus" as the finale and the audience dispersed.

John Howard Payne had returned at last to his "Home Sweet Home."

10.

I'LL TAKE YOU HOME AGAIN, KATHLEEN

"Homesick, darling?" Thomas Westendorf asked his lovely wife. She gazed across the vast expanse of the blue Atlantic, sighed wearily and answered, "You know I am, Thomas. You know how I feel way down deep inside." "Only too well," he said. "The roses have left your cheeks and your eyes are heavy with tears. And I wonder sometimes if you love me at all."

She reached over and took his hands in hers. "You know I love you, Thomas, almost more than life itself. But I want to get back to Bowling Green. I'm homesick for the trees and the old streets and the familiar sights that even seem to haunt my dreams now that we're so far from home." "And homesick for the little grave in the cemetery on Milford Street," he continued. "Yes, Thomas, dreadfully homesick. I want so much to kneel again on the clean rich earth where our precious baby was buried. Oh, why can't the ship go faster, Thomas? Why must it sail so slowly when my heart is breaking and my life seems to be slowly ebbing away?"

Thomas rose, pulled his deck chair closer, put his strong arm gently about her shoulder and drew her closer to him. "I'll take you home, Kathleen, as rapidly as I can. I've lost my child, as have you, but I don't think I could stand losing you, too, darling. That's almost more than a man could bear. I'll take you to our beloved Bowling Green in Virginia just as quickly as I can." She leaned heavily upon him and soon dropped off to sleep. Sitting there on the deck of the ship that was taking them home from a brief European visit, Thomas Westendorf reviewed the happy as well as the tragic incidents that they had shared prior

46

to that moment. He had been born in the lovely village of Bowling Green, Va. on February 23, 1848. In his mind's eye he could see the house that stood at the foot of Anderson Ave. where he had spent the happy and carefree days of his boyhood. He recalled the visits to historic Richmond, thirty-four miles to the south, and that memorable trip to Washington, D.C. seventy-two miles to the north. The beautiful trees, spacious lawns and comfortable homes of the village were well known throughout the Old Dominion. There he had grown into young manhood, surrounded by loving relatives and devoted friends. And there he had met Kathleen, as charming and as lovely a young woman as the south had ever seen. He thought of their courtship and recalled the long walks in the twilight that took them past the Kilwinning-Crosse Lodge, the second oldest Masonic Lodge established in America. He remembered the walk they had taken one afternoon out to the Garrett Farm, seven miles northeast of the town, where John Wilkes Booth hid after assassinating President Lincoln, and where he is said to have been slain. Then there were the visits to the Old Mansion, the town's oldest house, memorable because of a huge banquet served on the lawn when General George Washington honored Lafayette, celebrating the surrender of Cornwallis and the dawn of freedom for the infant Republic.

He recalled the afternoon of their marriage in famous old St. Asaph Church, the last parish set up by the government of Virginia before the separation of Church and State, and sold by the Episcopalians to the Methodists after the Civil War. The radiance of that day when they pledged their love each to the other still glowed warmly in his heart. Little did they dream when they said those words "till death us do part" that death was so soon to visit them. But there in Bowling Green their baby was born and there, after a short illness, the child died and was buried. And with her child's death, something died inside of Kathleen. Westendorf took a leave of absence from his position as a teacher of music to children in public as well as reform schools, and persuaded his wife to go with him on a European trip, hoping

47

she would regain her health and return home strengthened and refreshed. But the remedy failed to work.

While they were sight-seeing in Germany, Kathleen turned to him one morning and said, "Thomas, I want to go home." "All right, darling," he replied. "We will pack up and take the first ship available." But even the anticipation of an early return left her heartsick and empty inside. Thomas tried to be as tender and considerate as a loving husband could, but he knew that his beloved had lost her will to live, and was actually resigned to her own death. While her love for him was great, the love she bore for her departed baby seemed even greater. She grew daily worse, mourning constantly for home. The sadness in her voice coupled with the anguish in her eyes were almost more than Thomas could bear. To ease the strain and tension of the long voyage home, and to lighten the burden that was pressing so heavily upon his own heart, he sat beside her on the deck one afternoon and wrote a song.

"It's all your very own, my sweet," he said, as he handed her a copy of the stanzas. She smiled, took the paper and began to read these words.

I'll take you home again, Kathleeen, Across the waters dark and wide,
To where your heart has ever been, Since first you were my bonny bride;
The roses all have left your cheeks; I've watched them fade away and die;
Your voice is sad whene'er you speak, And tears bedim your loving eye.

I know you love me, Kathleen dear; Your heart was ever fond and true;
I always feel when you are near, That life holds nothing, dear, but you.
The smiles that once you gave to me, I scarcely ever see them now,

48

Though many, many times I see A darkening shadow on your brow.

To that dear home beyond the sea, My Kathleen shall again return,
And when thy old friends welcome thee, Thy loving heart will cease to yearn.
Where laughs the little silver stream Beside your mother's humble cot,
And brightest rays of sunshine gleam, There all your grief will be forgot.

Oh, I will take you back, Kathleen, To where your heart will feel no pain;
And when the fields are fresh and green, I'll take you to your home again.

"Oh, it's beautiful," she whispered. "But I don't think I'll ever gaze upon those fresh fields or see those loving friends again, Thomas. I don't think I'll live to reach Virginia." "Darling, please," he pleaded. "And, oh, darling," she continued, "forgive me if I seem to have forgotten how to smile and try to understand why there's a darkening shadow on my brow." "I loved the baby, too, Kathleen," he whispered, "I loved the baby, too. So please don't torture me like this, darling." But his pleadings were in vain. Nourishment, medicine, love and tender care were to no avail. Kathleen slowly wasted away and died aboard ship. After solemn services were held by the Captain, she was buried at sea. Before the vessel landed on the shores of the new world, Thomas P. Westendorf had written down the words and music of his one song that was to become immortal.

Returning to Bowling Green, Va. in 1900, he published "I'll Take You Home Again, Kathleen," and that same year sold his home and the other pieces of property he owned. He published only one edition of the new ballad and then forgot to take out a copyright to protect his interests as author and composer. The pastor of the local Methodist Church at that time was a Rev. Mr. Rowe, whose daughter, Nettie, knew Mr. Westendorf well. To her he gave an autographed copy of the song as a keepsake. She married a Mr. Richards, a Steward in the same church, and this valuable autographed copy passed into the hands of their daughter, Mrs. Alice Richards DeJarnette. It is now kept in the Henry Ford Museum, Detroit, Michigan.

Westendorf, heartbroken after the deaths of his baby and his wife, moved to Georgia between 1900 and 1905, and there he died. As the personal favorite of the great electrician and inventor, Thomas Alva Edison, this song was sung at his funeral. As a tribute to Edison, Henry Ford made photostatic copies of Mrs. DeJarnette's autographed copy and distributed them among his friends.

So out of the joy of one great love and the agony of one great loss, Thomas Westendorf wrote his one famous song that has earned for itself a rightful place in the annals of American music.

11.

JINGLE BELLS

"Jingle Bells" is one song that was not written by the man to whom most people give the credit. The name of the author-composer is always given as merely J. Pierpont, which leads many folks to the erroneous conclusion that there was some connection between him and the family of the wealthy business tycoon, sometimes called one of the nation's "robber barons," J. Pierpont Morgan.

Starting from there, they soon discover that the said successful financier was the son of Juliet Pierpont Morgan, who was the second daughter of the Rev. John Pierpont, from whom the future baby took his name. All of this intriguing background leads to further interesting research regarding the said clergyman, and soon we learn that he was born in Litchfield, Connecticut, April 6, 1785, educated at Yale, tutored for a while in New Haven and finally went to Charleston, South Carolina as a tutor to a wealthy southern family. Following his teaching days, he tried his hands variously at such jobs as a partner in a drygoods store in Boston as well as in Baltimore, where he married the sister of his third partner, Joseph Lord, in 1810.

There followed a period of poverty when the family was forced to sell its silver piece by piece to keep from starving, which could well have motivated the famous grandson to amass his tremendous fortune. Anyway it was during these trying times that daughter Juliet was born. Having failed as a business man, Pierpont decided to take up preaching, so he entered Harvard Divinity School in 1816, paying expenses by writing and plugging his book, "Airs of Palestine." There followed some years as a controversial minister in the Unitarian Church, after which he settled down to a twenty-six-year pastorate, serving the Hollis Street Unitarian congregation in Boston. He was known as a controversialist all his life, as well as a vigorous opponent of slavery and intemperance, until finally ousted from his pulpit in 1840.

He published a book, "Poems and Hymns" that year, including in its pages a hymn still used at the laying of church cornerstones, "On this stone now laid with prayer." Other pastorates in other states followed until he became a chaplain in the Army at the outbreak of the Civil War. Following that labor of love, he served a political appointment for some years, passing away at the age of eighty-one, on August 27, 1866, leaving as his literary legacy his two books, the second of which went through another edition as late as 1854.

That such a remarkable, versatile and unusual man should have had the talent to write "Jingle Bells" would make an interesting story, to say the least. But, alas, although many writers say he did, the facts are that he did not, and he would be the first to clarify the issue, were he still alive.

A letter of inquiry addressed to the Pierpont Morgan Library, 33 East Thirty-sixth Street, New York, 16, soon straightens us out. For the librarian replies, "I have no record that the Rev. John Pierpont (1785-1866) was the author of Jingle Bells, nor that any other John Pierpont in the Morgan family was," which soon takes care of that.

A letter to the Library of Congress, through the courtesy of one's State Senator, provides additional data to the effect that, "In our collections we have a copy of this song which was published and copyrighted by the Boston firm, Oliver Ditson and Company, in 1857. The copyright was renewed by J. Pierpont in 1885, which would seem to eliminate Rev. John Pierpont as the composer, since, according to a biographical sketch of him which is to be found on page 875 of Julian's 'Dictionary of Hymnology,' London, 1915, he died in 1866. Additional information in the Copyright Office, however, completely rules out

John Pierpont as the composer, because the J. Pierpont is identified as James S. Pierpont."

To one who had ransacked the biographies of J. Pierpont Morgan and had finally come across the name of an Aunt Fanny, this came as a distinct shock. Doesn't the second stanza of the song tell about somebody taking Miss Fanny Bright for a ride? It does, but there must have been many Aunt Fannys a century ago. So we are back where we started, with a relatively unknown James S. Pierpont, who composed quite a few selections now copyrighted in his name in the Library of Congress, but of whom comparatively little is known except that he has had the dubious honor of being confused with the scion of one of America's richest families, when all the time he had won the distinction of having written one of the most delightful winter songs of all time, and one that will continue to be a source of merriment and delight to children at Christmas for centuries to come. At least, it is comforting to know who didn't write "Jingle Bells," whether we ever know who did and why, or not!!

12.

KEEP THE HOME FIRES BURNING

"Tipperary, Tipperary, that's all I hear and I'm fed up with it," Mrs. Clara Davies said to her handsome son, Ivor. The talented twenty-one-year-old youth tried to calm her down. "Don't get excited over it, Mother. It's not such a bad song at that," he said. "And it's shot through and through with dear old London and what more does a Britisher want?"

"I've just heard it so often I'm getting tired of it, bored with it," she explained. "Tipperary, Picadilly, Leicester Square, you can have them. I've had all I can stand."

"Just a minute, Mother," Ivor pleaded. "Give the composer the benefit of the doubt. After all, he wrote the song on a bet just two years ago. You must give him credit for doing a good job, even if it's being sung too often for your comfort."

Young Ivor Novello, who dropped his last name, Davies, when he decided that a name he had recently heard, Novello, sounded more artistic, was right. Two years earlier, in 1912, an ex-fishmonger, Jack Judge, made a bet with a friend that he could write a song and produce it on the same day. "Tipperary" became an immediate success, gaining a sizeable fortune for the composer, despite the fact that its constant use was something of a headache to Mrs. Davies. Ivor's mother, though, kept insisting, "A good song ought to be more dignified. Tipperary is too flighty." So she began to goad her son into doing something about it. She had great confidence in her gifted offspring. As a doting mother she boasted that the lad cried in perfect thirds. As he grew into boyhood she constantly reminded him that "time was short" and "if you're ever going to amount to anything, you'd better begin. I want promise to become performance."

Then came the war, and soon men were being herded into army camps like cattle. After drill, while they were nursing their sore feet and soothing aching muscles, they would talk of home with its comforts and conveniences as well as its precious memories. When they left England to invade the continent, they sang "Tipperary" as if it represented the last link to that which they all held dear. Ivor Novello, just twenty-one, blessed with a profile that rivalled that of John Barrymore, at his mother's request sat down at the piano and wrote his reply to "Tipperary" in a song which began, "Keep the home fires burning." It didn't affect the sales or the popularity of the other song, although it was destined to become one of the most popular songs ever written, much to the chagrin of his regular publisher who did not think the ditty worth printing, and rejected it in no uncertain terms. Judge had done it at thirty-four, but Novello beat him at his own game, writing his masterpiece the year he reached his majority. Standing on the pinnacle of success there is no direction to go but down, and Ivor had reached the top too early for his own good. If he couldn't stay there, he could only go in one direction.

The success of his song made him a national idol overnight. His handsome profile became that of the ideal soldier to every mother and sweetheart and wife, and he soon found himself the symbol of English manhood at its highest and best. An invitation to appear in the movies was inevitable, and his cinema success, "The Call of the Blood," made him the star of 1920. Not content to dramatize roles created by other authors, he dipped his pen into the bottle of ink and produced "The Rat" in which he played the leading role, billing himself as "author, producer, director and featured actor."

Straight dramatic roles soon gave way to musicales, and "Glamorous Night" was a hit, eclipsed only by his fourth show,

55

"The Dancing Years," which ran successfully for ten years. In all, he wrote ten musicales, giving Britons the kind of entertainment and music they longed for. Although not as well known in America as his fellow-artist Noel Coward, he was far more popular in England, almost unanimously conceded the honor of being "the most considerable personality on the English stage."

The coming of the Second World War frightened songwriters. This business of killing on a huge scale, coupled with the annihilation of cities during night bombing raids, to say nothing of the A-bomb, wasn't worth singing about. So Novello produced nothing to compare with his 1914 success, "Keep the home fires burning." He did get his name in the papers, though, but not in the way he planned. A knighthood was denied him, a disappointment he shared with Coward, but there was some compensation in the fact that his mother was made a Dame of the British Empire, for her success as leader of a famous Welsh choir. The "Great Profile," however, was accused of plotting with an infatuated girl to get gasoline to which he was not entitled, to drive around in his swanky Rolls-Royce. Still strikingly handsome at fifty, he heard himself sentenced to four weeks in jail. His female admirers could hardly believe their ears when the verdict was pronounced, but they stood by and cheered their idol as he was led away to serve his sentence in England's gloomy Wormwood Scrubbs prison. While the women wailed outside the prison walls, Ivor thought that a curse must rest on the name he had taken years ago from a "lush music hall singer, Miss Novello."

But he did his time and soon was released to resume the lavish living to which he had become accustomed at his spacious country mansion "Red Roofs." "My ambition," he said on one occasion, "is to go on working till I drop. I should like to make an enchanting curtain speech at the end of a wildly successful first night, and, to the sound of cheers and applause, drop gracefully dead. If possible, before the curtain falls."

One night in March, 1951, his fifty-eighth year, his wish was almost granted. Three hours after the close of a brilliant performance of his new musicale, "Kings Rhapsody," he died of a heart attack. Maybe then he caught a glimpse of the "silver lining through the dark cloud shining" which had been denied him here below.

13.

LITTLE ANNIE ROONEY

The incongruities of the song-writing business are almost beyond belief. For example, the Russian born British song-writer, Herman Darweski, who died in 1947 at the age of sixty-four, didn't stutter, but he certainly inspired his fellow countrymen to when he dashed off the first World War favorite, "K-K-K-Katy." In fact, this unusual man was at one time the piano teacher of Princess, later Queen, Elizabeth. But this isn't the first recorded instance of a popular song-writer rubbing elbows with royalty. Lady Arthur Hill, who composed "In the Gloaming," was the widow of Lord Arthur Hill, comptroller of Queen Victoria's household, which is about as close to Buckingham Palace as one can get. She passed away in 1944 at her home in East Hampstead Park, Berkshire, in her ninety-fifth year.

As for the wailing notes of "The Prisoner's Song," which earned Vernon Dalhart and his cousin, Guy Massey, a cool million in royalties, neither man had served time behind the bars which they made famous in their most popular hill-billy ballad. The only reason they wrote and recorded the song in the first place was because the Victor Talking Machine Company wanted something to put on the back of their recording of "The Wreck of the Old 97."

As for "The Trail of the Lonesome Pine," which Ballard McDonald and Harry Carroll immortalized in their 1913 song hit, forty years after John Fox had done the same thing in a novel bearing the identical title, tourists are always disappointed when they discover that there is really no such tree. It existed only in the fertile imagination of a novelist who did his job so well that over a million copies of his book were sold. The citizens of Big Stone Gap, Virginia, have either been trying to find the tree or apologizing for its non-existence ever since.

All of this introduces the disillusioning fact that the popular song of yesteryear, "Little Annie Rooney" was not written by a love sick youth for his pretty gingham-gowned, blonde-braided schoolgirl sweetheart. Annie, strange as it may seem, was a wee little tyke just fourteen months old when she inspired the song that became a popular favorite in the closing decades of the nineteenth century. Annie, who became Mrs. Eric M. Erickson, issued a call in 1955 from her home in Fairhaven, Massachusetts.

"I am interested," she said, "in finding out what happened to my mother's cousin who made my name so famous. If he is living, he is probably in his nineties, but he might still be living. Members of my mother's family lived to a great old age. All that I know of are gone now, but I thought perhaps someone in England might have known the composer Michael Nolan, and I might get in touch with some of the family again."

Mrs. Erickson went on to explain that her father, William Rooney, used to bounce her on his knee while he sang, "She's my sweetheart, I'm her beau." Then he would tell her, "Annie, never forget that's your song." And John Nolan, Michael's brother, would constantly remind her, "Mike composed that song just for you, little Annie Rooney."

A few years after Nolan wrote the ditty that became a London music hall favorite, the Rooneys packed up and left England for the United States, settling in Providence, Rhode Island. With the broad Atlantic separating them from British relatives, the different branches of the family soon lost touch with each other, but the song lived on. Mrs. Erickson, a frail, white-haired composer herself, added these words, "I still remember my first day at school. I wouldn't tell the teacher my name, and then I burst into tears when the little boy behind me said, 'Her name is Annie Rooney.'" Mrs. Erickson, a native of Oldham, England, died on Friday, August 15, 1958 in New Bedford, Massachusetts, at the age of seventy-three. In addition to being the inspiration for a successful song, she became a composer herself, writing more than thirty-three published compositions before her death.

Whether she finds Michael Nolan remains to be seen, but the popularity of the song which she inspired as a tiny baby is assured.

14.

LORENA

Eleanor Blocksom burst into tears. "But I love him, Daddy; I love him and I want to marry him," she cried.

"Bah!" shouted her father. "Love! What do you know about love? Nothing. It's just infatuation. That's what it is, infatuation."

"It's not, Daddy. I'm the one who ought to know," Eleanor insisted. But her father was adamant. "I know what's best for you, dear; I'm your father. And I'm not going to have my daughter, a Blocksom, throw her life away by marrying a poor country preacher. I'm not going to have it, and the sooner you understand that, the better."

Eleanor fled from the room, ran upstairs and threw herself upon her bed, bathing the counterpane with her tears. Her mother hurried up after her, sat on the edge of the bed beside her and tried to say a few words of comfort.

"But you and Daddy don't understand, Mother. I'm no baby and Harry's no infant. We're both grown up and we're in love and we want to get married," Eleanor pleaded. Sitting up, she looked into her mother's eyes. "Don't you understand, Mother?" Her mother nodded her head. "I understand, darling. But Daddy is a proud man, and he's afraid that after a few years you will tire of Harry and come creeping back home, and he wants to spare you the embarrassment and the humiliation," she said.

"Tire of love? Do you actually mean that, Mother? Are you tired of Daddy? And is he tired of you?" Eleanor shouted.

"But darling, try to look at it this way. You are used to comforts and luxuries that a poor preacher could never afford to give you. And you've been brought up in an educational and

61

cultural atmosphere that are now so much a part of your life that you take them for granted. When you begin to long for all of those things after a few years of marriage, then what?" her mother asked.

"And if I have all that and lose love, what have I left?" Eleanor argued.

Downstairs, Mr. Blocksom paced the floor of the large, spacious living room. "I wish that young preacher, that Mr. Webster, had never come to Zanesville," he muttered to himself. "How did I know he had eyes for Eleanor when he kept coming here day after day?" His wife soon joined him and they went into the kitchen together. Mrs. Blocksom explained, "Eleanor is quite upset, darling. She insists she is very much in love with the young minister."

"She'll get over it, dear. Don't worry. I think I know what's best for our children, and Eleanor's my favorite." The conversation drifted to the day the new pastor had come to the struggling Church at Zanesville, Ohio, just before the Civil War. He had been attracted to the Blocksoms almost immediately, since they were one of the leading families not only in community life but also in the activities of the little Church. In addition, Eleanor sang in the choir, which caused him to take a second, as well as a third and fourth glance in her direction. Soon he discovered that their home was the center of many activities, and he found more excuses for visiting there in the interests of the Church as well as the community. And, as was inevitable, Rev. H. D. L. Webster and Eleanor Blocksom fell in love.

Added to the vigorous objections of her father were the protests of one of her sisters. "Eleanor," her sister said over and over again, "can't you see the folly of leaving a wealthy and aristocratic home and tying yourself down with a poor, struggling preacher?"

"No, I can't," Eleanor answered. "When you love someone as I love Harry, money doesn't mean everything."

"Well, it may not mean much to you, but it does to me and

Daddy and I won't have you throwing your life away like this," her sister added. So, just when everyone thought the wedding date would be announced, the family "ganged up" on Eleanor. She received what amounted to an ultimatum from them. "If you marry him, we will disinherit you," she was told, in no uncertain terms. "So tell the Rev. Mr. Webster that it is all over between you."

That night the young couple met for their last date. The young pastor and his sweetheart stood on a hill overlooking Zanesville and spoke their tragic farewells. Pointing to a spot nearby, Eleanor said, "Darling, there's where the log hut stood. Betty Zane went up there with a cask of gunpowder in her apron during the Indian attack, September 27, 1777, and, for her daring and bravery, the town honored her by taking her name. I wish I were as brave. If I were, I'd tell Daddy and Mother and the rest of them goodbye, and run away with you."

He put his arm about her and they stood near the summit in the moonlight. "I wouldn't want you to do that, darling. The day would come when you would long to see them again, and I would always feel down in my heart that you held it against me for insisting that you disown them and marry me."

"But I love you, Harry. You know I love you," she said.

"I know you love me, Eleanor, and I know that I love you, and I know that our love is all that matters in the world. But I have a Church and you have a family, and if I ran away, that would be the end of my ministry. Then what would we do? You would always feel that you had made me give up the one thing that I want to do more than anything else in all the world. You'd feel that way about my ministry and I'd feel the same way about your family. And it would create a gulf between us. Then what would happen to our love?"

"I don't know, Harry; I don't know," she replied. "I only know that you love me and I love you and nothing else matters." He kissed her tenderly and they clung together in a moment of ecstasy, as if trying to blot out all the world and all the questions that had no answers and all the future that loomed so empty and desolate and lonely before them. Then she returned his ring, and they walked silently to her home, too heart-heavy to speak, each praying for a miracle that would never happen. Realizing that his ministry in the community was over with the breaking of his engagement, Webster went west, trying to forget by giving himself to the service of the pioneers of the rapidly expanding frontier. Later he tried to resolve his heartache by writing a poem in which he told of his disappointment in love. In order not to embarrass his beloved, he took the letters of her name and created the name "Lorena" and penned what became the most famous love-song for heart-broken lovers of that era.

The years creep slowly by, Lorena; The snow is on the grass
    again;
The sun's low down the sky, Lorena; The frost gleams where
    the flowers have been.
But the heart throbs on as warmly now, As when the summer
    days were nigh,
Oh! the sun can never dip so low Adown affection's cloudless
    sky.

A hundred months have passed, Lorena, Since last I held that
    hand in mine;
And felt that pulse beat fast, Lorena, Though mine beat faster
    far than thine;
A hundred months. 'Twas flowery May, When up the hilly slope
    we climbed,
To watch the dying of the day And hear the distant Church
    bells chime.

It matters little now, Lorena, The past is in the eternal past,
Our heads will soon lie low, Lorena; Life's tide is ebbing out so
    fast;
There is a future, Oh, thank God; Of life this is so small a part;
'Tis dust to dust beneath the sod; But there, up there, 'tis heart
    to heart.

Later still, J. B. Webster, composer of the music for the gospel song "The Sweet Bye and Bye" and no kin to the poet, set the words to music. When published, the song became an immediate success. More than likely, Eleanor never knew she was Lorena, but whether she ever forgot the one great love of her life has never been determined.

15.

MARY HAD A LITTLE LAMB

The Secretary of State nodded. "Yes, Mrs. Hale," he said, "the President will see you in a few moments."

"Thank you, Mr. Seward," the distinguished seventy-five-year-old woman replied. "This is an hour I have been looking forward to for many years. I hope the President will be impressed with my proposal and in a responsive mood."

"I am sure he will be, Mrs. Hale. Mr. Lincoln is an open-minded man, and, with your powers of persuasion, I have no doubt as to the outcome," Mr. Seward said. A short while later, one of the Presidential secretaries invited them into Mr. Lincoln's office in the White House. It was a hot afternoon in October, 1863, and the President seemed to be bearing not only the weight of the tragic Civil War, but also the weight of the entire world on his shoulders as he rose, greeted his Secretary of State, and stepped from behind his desk to meet their visitor. Mr. Seward introduced her. "Mr. President, Mrs. Sara Josepha Hale."

They shook hands, after which Mr. Lincoln motioned to a chair. "Sit down, please, Mrs. Hale. Your visit is a distinct honor. It isn't often a President has such an opportunity to get the low-down on the latest fashions."

"Then you read Godey's 'Ladies' Magazine,' Mr. Lincoln?" she asked, curiously.

The President laughed as he and Mr. Seward sat down nearby. "Heavens no, Mrs. Hale," he said. "But I know you by reputation as its editor. Mrs. Lincoln is the one who keeps up with the latest fashions, and when she saw your name on the list of today's appointments, she asked me to give you her greetings. And she posted me on who you were and how important your journal is in the world of women's fashions. They call you a fashion dictator, do they not?"

"Oh, no, Mr. Lincoln," protested Mrs. Hale. "A fashion editor, yes; but not a dictator."

As the conversation continued, Mrs. Hale explained the real reason for her visit.

"Mr. Lincoln," she said, "for many years I have tried to interest American leaders in a pet project of mine. I want all of us in these United States to celebrate together an annual day of Thanksgiving on a certain day every year. It would become as important a day as Christmas, or Valentine's Day or even the Fourth of July."

"But we do have Thanksgiving days, Mrs. Hale," explained Mr. Lincoln. "In fact, last August sixth I signed a proclamation asking our people to set aside September twenty-sixth as a day of thanksgiving."

"It was to celebrate a military victory, was it not, Mr. President?"

"Why, yes. Why do you ask?" the President inquired.

"Because I feel we should have a national day of thanksgiving to be observed apart from military victories or defeats. It should be a day on which all of us as Americans would thank God for all His blessings, in a united gesture of gratitude. To that end I have called upon Congressmen, Governors, Public officials, and have written countless letters, articles and editorials. I even spoke to your predecessors in office, Presidents Fillmore, Pierce and Buchanan. They gave me little encouragement and no support," she continued.

Mr. Seward interrupted, "And she has given me no rest, Mr. Lincoln. She just *had* to see you because she felt you would do something about it at last."

"Just what do you want me to do, Mrs. Hale," the President asked.

She answered, "Set aside the fourth Thursday in November as a national day of thanksgiving, and urge that this holiday be celebrated annually by all of our people."

Mr. Seward broke into the conversation again. "Mr. Lincoln, you may be interested in knowing that Mrs. Hale not only writes editorials and letters, but poems as well."

"Interesting," the President commented.

"And one of her poems happens to be a children's favorite all over the country," Mr. Seward added.

Mr. Lincoln looked up. "Yes?" he said. "Which one?"

Mrs. Hale smiled. "Mr. President, I am not going to pressure you into doing something just because of the popularity of one of my poems."

"I know, Mrs. Hale. But you have my curiosity aroused," Mr. Lincoln added.

"In that case," suggested Mr. Seward, "you'd better tell him."

Mrs. Hale smiled. "Back in 1830—that's thirty-three years ago—this poem appeared in a book I prepared entitled 'Juvenile Miscellany.' While gathering interesting material for the volume, I came across the story of a little girl up in Massachusetts whose name was Mary. When she was a very small girl, her father found a new-born lamb out in the barn which had been deserted by its mother. He took the little thing into the kitchen of their home, and cared for it until it was strong enough to look after itself. During those weeks, little Mary became so attached to the little lamb that she wouldn't let it out of her sight."

Mr. Lincoln smiled. "Don't tell me," he broke in, "that Mary took the lamb to school with her."

Mrs. Hale nodded. "She did just that, Mr. President, to the consternation of the teacher and the delight of the pupils. They were inseparable, you see, and wherever Mary went, the lamb went; and wherever the lamb went, Mary went."

"So you," the President said, pointing a long bony finger at Mrs. Hale, "are the author of 'Mary had a little lamb.' "

Mrs. Hale held up her right hand and smiled. "Guilty, your honor," she said.

"And for the author of such a children's favorite, a President should do most anything, to show his appreciation as well as his respect," Mr. Lincoln added.

"I'd settle for a proclamation setting aside the fourth Thursday in November as a national day of thanksgiving and prayer," Mrs. Hale replied.

After her departure, Mr. Lincoln picked up a pen and began to write. Toward the bottom of the page he penned these words, "I do therefore invite my fellow-citizens in every part of the United States and also those who are at sea and those who sojourn in foreign lands, to set apart and observe the last Thursday in November as a day of thanksgiving and praise to our beneficent Father who dwelleth in the heavens." The proclamation of 1863 was followed by a similar one the very next year, thus establishing a precedent for the entire nation.

The Congress took no official action on the matter until President Franklin D. Roosevelt attempted to change the date to an earlier one in 1939. Due to the controversy over this move to shift the date of the holiday, the Congress passed a resolution in December, 1941, making the fourth Thursday in November a legal Thanksgiving holiday for the United States of America.

Had she lived that long, Sara Josepha Hale, author of 'Mary had a little lamb,' would have been thrilled. Its immortality had been guaranteed, however, in 1877, when Thomas Alva Edison quoted the poem as he recorded sound for the first time in human history in the first record ever made.

16.

MARYLAND MY MARYLAND

"Come in," said the twenty-two-year-old professor, when he heard a knock at his door. It was early evening, during the last week in April, 1861. The door opened and several students entered his room on the campus of Poydras College, situated on the Fausse Riviere, about thirty miles above Baton Rouge, Louisiana.

"Are we disturbing you, Professor Randall?" one of the young men asked.

"Not at all," the English teacher replied. "Come in, please, and sit down. I was just reading some poems written by the Irish poet, James Clarence Mangan." When the boys were comfortably seated, another student said, "I don't believe I've ever heard of him, Professor. What did he write?"

James Ryder Randall, widely-travelled graduate of Georgetown College, picked up a slender volume from his desk. "Mangan was a strange Irishman. Before his death in 1849 he wrote some stirring patriotic verses as well as some rather melancholy ones. Take this one, for instance. It's one of my favorites, because of the unusual meter in which it is written.

'I see thee ever in my dreams, Karaman!
Thy hundred hills, thy thousand streams, Karaman, O Karaman!
As when thy gold-bright morning gleams, As when the deepening sunset seams
With lines of light thy hills and streams, Karaman!' "

"It's like 'Tannenbaum, O Tannenbaum' or 'Christmas Tree, O Christmas Tree,' isn't it, Professor?" asked another. "Yes,"

Randall replied. "Both are written in the same strange meter."

The conversation soon turned to the purpose of the student's visits, and the young men asked their English teacher about the man for whom the college was named.

"His full name was Julien De Lalande Poydras," the young faculty member explained. "As a young and handsome man, he fell deeply in love with a girl during the Mardi Gras many years ago. She came from a very poor family, and realized she could not bring a dowry to her wedding, so she fled from her lover and never saw him again. Poydras searched far and wide but never found her. When he died in 1824, at seventy-eight, he left in his will a sum of $30,000 each for Pointe Coupee and West Baton Rouge parishes in Louisiana, the income of which was to provide dowries for poor girls when they married. Furthermore, in his will he also left a provision providing for the freeing of his slaves and for the pensioning of all slaves over sixty. If other wealthy land-owners had done that, this tragic war could have been averted."

A discussion of slavery followed, the teacher and students commenting on the gravity of the situation that faced both the north and the south in the months ahead.

"We'll knock those Yankees out in thirty days," one particularly belligerent youth boasted.

"Don't be too sure about that," their teacher cautioned. "Every war begins with each side thinking it can quickly subdue the other, but most wars bog down and last year after year until both sides ultimately lose, regardless of which one wins the military victory. Remember these dates; February 4, Confederate States formed; February 9, Jefferson Davis elected first president; February 18, inaugurated at Montgomery, Alabama, and again, on February 22, at Richmond; April 12, after authority had been wired to General Beauregard, the firing on Fort Sumter began; April 14, the surrender of the Fort."

"But we have Lee and Jackson," protested one of the students, "and hearts that will never surrender. But what about your state, Maryland, Professor? Where will she throw her strength? Which side will she line up with?"

Randall spoke up. "I was born in Baltimore, and I know Maryland will do the right thing. She always has and she always will; of that I am confident. The state of Charles Carroll of Carrollton, signer of the Declaration of Independence, and the state of John Eager Howard, Revolutionary soldier, governor and distinguished senator, will do the right thing."

At that moment another student burst excitedly into the room, a newspaper in his hand. "Professor Randall," he said, "here's the latest copy of the 'Delta.' The news isn't too good."

As the others crowded around, the young teacher, a direct descendant of Rene Leblanc, who was immortalized in the poem 'Evangeline,' began to scan the paper hurriedly for news of his native Maryland. He found an article quickly and began to read: "Baltimore, Maryland, April 19, 1861. On Wednesday, April 16, 1861, the Sixth Massachusetts Infantry left Boston for Washington. On Saturday, April 19, the soldiers reached Baltimore, and started to march for the Camden Street station to entrain for the capital city, when shots were fired by radical southern sympathizers. Baltimore is in a frenzy—Southerners crowd the streets to ridicule the soldiers—firing—a desperate battle—three soldiers killed—some twenty wounded—nine citizens slain—more wounded—." Randall looked up. "It can't be," he said in a half-whisper. "Not in Maryland. It can't be. Innocent men and women dying from shots fired at them by their own fellow-countrymen."

One of the students said, "But it's true. It says so, Professor, right here in the paper."

"Believe me," Randall continued, "Maryland won't take that lying down. She's no coward. When she wakens, this giant among states, this mighty man of valor, will fight for her rights and defend them to the last man."

The boys talked heatedly about enlisting right away, and soon left to go to their rooms, pack their belongings and hurry to the nearest recruiting station. "We'll be back by commencement time in June, Professor," they called back with the enthusiasm of idealistic youth. "The war will be all over then. Goodbye."

Randall watched them go, and then picked up the paper to reread the account of tragic events in Baltimore. With the strange meter of 'Karaman' beating in his mind and the news from his native state stirring in his heart, he began to write a poem of his own, crying out to his people to avenge the tragedy that had taken place in the streets of her largest city, and make amends before their fellow Americans. His stirring poem began with these dramatic lines:

The despot's heel is on thy shore, Maryland.
His torch is at thy temple door, Maryland.
Avenge the patriotic gore, That flecked the streets of Baltimore,
And be the battle-queen of yore. Maryland, my Maryland.

Thou wilt not cower in the dust, Maryland.
Thy beaming sword shall never rust, Maryland.
Remember Carroll's sacred trust, Remember Howard's warlike thrust,
And all thy slumberers with the just, Maryland, my Maryland.

Stanza gave way to stanza until the last, the ninth, read as follows:

I hear the distant thunder hum, Maryland.
The Old Line's bugle, fife and drum, Maryland.
She is not dead, nor deaf, nor dumb. Huzza! She spurns the Northern scum!
She breathes! She burns! She'll come! She'll come! Maryland, my Maryland.

Barred by physical disabilities from engaging in actual combat, Randall worked with several southern newspapers. After some years as secretary to a Congressman and a Senator from Georgia, he died in August, January 14, 1908, his sixty-ninth year. This one poem, called "The Marseillaise" of the Confederacy, outlived all of his other subsequent labors.

17.

O COLUMBIA, THE GEM OF THE OCEAN

"It's amazing, perfectly amazing," Mr. Harford said to his guests that morning in the living room of his Decatur Street home in Philadelphia.

"What do you mean, Dad?" his twenty-year-old daughter asked, rather puzzled.

"The coincidence, dear," her father replied.

"What coincidence?" she asked, a bit insistently.

"Well," Mr. Harford began, "when these two gentlemen came knocking at our door a few minutes ago, we had no idea what they wanted, did we?"

"Why no," she replied.

"But when they stated the reason for their visit, I couldn't help but think back to a similar incident which took place right here in Philadelphia in 1798," her father continued.

"Since this is 1843, and the other incident took place forty-five years ago, what has that to do with Mr. á Becket and Mr. Shaw?" she asked, pointing to the two young men who were seated near the piano.

Mr. á Becket interrupted, "You have my curiosity aroused too, Mr. Harford. What's on your mind?"

Mr. Harford smiled. "If I remember correctly, Mr. á Becket," he began, "you told us that you were an actor at the Chestnut Street Theatre, and that your friend, Mr. Shaw, was a singer over at the Chinese Museum."

"That's right, Mr. Harford," his guest replied.

"And you went on to explain that Mr. Shaw came to you early this morning, requesting you to help him write a new song," Mr. Harford continued.

"Correct again," Mr. á Becket answered. "Shaw wanted me to help him write a new patriotic song, to give his program a lift or a bang or a shot in the arm," he continued, "but there was so much confusion at the theatre that I asked the manager where we could go to find a quiet room with a good piano, and he gave us your name and address. So here we are," the young actor explained.

"That's what is so strange, Mr. á Becket," Mr. Harford said. "Because back in '98, there was another actor in Philadelphia, a twenty-eight-year-old youth by the name of Gilbert Fox."

"Never heard of him," á Becket interrupted.

"No," added his host; "that was before your day. Anyway, this Mr. Fox went to Joseph Hopkinson late one Saturday night and begged him to write a new patriotic song for a concert the following Monday night."

"He didn't give him much time, did he?" Shaw remarked.

"Not much, Mr. Shaw," Mr. Harford continued, "but Hopkinson took the strains of a martial air known as 'The President's March' and hammered out the thrilling stanzas of the well-known patriotic hymn 'Hail Columbia, happy land!' He gave the stanzas to his friend on Sunday afternoon and Fox introduced the song on Monday night. It went over with such a bang that President Adams and his cabinet attended one performance in a body, so great was the influence of the new song. And here are you two gentlemen, one an actor and one a musician, coming into our home with the same thing in mind."

"I have no illusions, Mr. Harford," á Becket explained. "Nor do I have the slightest intention of writing anything as dramatic as 'Hail Columbia.' That's a gem."

Mr. Shaw interrupted. "Wasn't Hopkinson the son of Francis Hopkinson, the musician and poet who signed the Declaration of Independence?" he asked.

"The very man," Mr. Harford said, "and if those two could do it, so can you."

Miss Harford broke into the conversation. "Samuel Smith was just twenty-three when he wrote 'My country, tis of thee'

75

back in 1832, and Francis Scott Key dashed off 'The star spangled banner' in a short while during the bombardment of Fort McHenry in 1814."

"But we have neither the bombardment nor the inspiration," Mr. Shaw explained. Miss Harford spoke up immediately. "Why not take the best of 'Hail Columbia,' 'America' and 'The star spangled banner' and make a new song all your very own?"

"And throw in the army and the navy for good measure," suggested her father. "But don't steal 'the land of the free and the home of the brave' from Key, because everyone will recognize it."

"You could use the same idea and express it in different words, though," Mr. á Becket suggested.

"For instance?" Shaw asked.

Mr. á Becket replied, "Say 'the home of the brave and the free,' and then add three cheers for the flag that flew over Fort McHenry, the inspiration of 'The star spangled banner.' In fact, you could almost say, 'The army and navy forever, Three cheers for the red, white and blue.' That's about as patriotic as you can get, without making the thing sickeningly sweet."

"The Germans always speak of their country as the fatherland, while we in America and those in England refer to their land as the motherland," commented Shaw. "So we made the word America the feminine of Americus, after the map-maker of Italy, Americus Vespicius, and Columbia the feminine form of Columbus, the discoverer."

"That reminds me of some lines from Timothy Dwight," Miss Harford added. "He wrote 'Columbia, Columbia, to glory arise, the queen of the world and the child of the skies,' "

"So we could begin our song, 'O Columbia, the gem of the ocean, The home of the brave and the free,' " Mr. à Becket added quickly. Sitting at the piano, picking out some melodies at random, á Becket soon had the group singing the refrain, "Three cheers for the red, white and blue." Turning to Shaw he said, "Get some paper and a pencil and take down these lines before I forget them." Playing and singing the new song simultaneously, as Shaw and Miss Harford wrote down the lines of the three stanzas, á Becket, in a short time, had composed his thrilling song "O Columbia, the gem of the ocean."

It was presented in public for the first time two days later, Shaw having the honor of singing it first, since it had been composed for his program at his request. The author and composer made no money from the new song, but was grateful that he, a native of England, had the honor of writing a patriotic song for his adopted country which enjoyed universal popularity and earned the unanimous acclaim of its people.

18.

ROCK-A-BYE BABY

"Effie; oh, Effie. Are you home?" the neighbour called.

Fifteen-year-old Effie Crockett called from the kitchen. "I'm back here. Come on in." Her friend walked through the house in Winthrop, Massachusetts, until she saw Effie washing dishes in the kitchen sink. "Oh, there you are. I wanted to see you before you went out."

"Well, sit down," Effie told her. "I'll be through here in a minute."

"Thanks, Effie, but I really don't have the time. I came over to see if you would look after the baby again this afternoon. I have a chance to go into town and there are several things I just have to do before the weekend. Are you available?"

Effie washed the last dish, hung up her wet dish towel, and dropped into a chair near the breakfast table. "You know me," she said. "Good old Effie Crockett, the world champion baby-sitter."

"That's sweet of you, Effie. I'll be leaving about three o'clock. I'll try to get the little darling to sleep before I go, but if I don't, I believe you can manage all right."

"I'll do my best," the young girl replied, as her neighbour returned hurriedly to her own home nearby.

A little later when Mrs. Crockett came home from the neighbourhood store laden down with packages and bundles, Effie told her the news. "What did you tell her, dear?" her mother asked.

"I told her I'd be there," Effie replied.

"You sound like a criminal going the last mile," her mother said, as she saw her daughter's sad expression and heard the doleful tone in her voice. "And your voice sounds like the voice of doom."

"If you knew that little brat—I mean, that little darling, like I do, you'd prefer walking the last mile to looking after him all afternoon. Of all the noisy, wiggling, disobedient, self-centered, stubborn little babies, this one takes the cake!"

"But think of the fun you'll have spending the money," her mother reminded her.

Effie smiled. "That's the only reason I'm going through with it, mother dear, as if you didn't already know."

"Just don't lose patience with the baby, Effie," her mother added, as she began to put some of the food away in the pantry nearby. "After all, we had our tough moments with you when you were small."

Effie laughed. "I don't doubt that a bit."

"In fact," her mother continued, "several times Daddy suggested that we put you in a little basket and leave you on the bank of the river for somebody else to find and take care of."

"Like the baby Moses?" Effie asked.

"Well, I believe that story gave him the idea," her mother continued.

"Just think of it, Mother," Effie said excitedly. "I could grow up to be a princess, just like Moses grew up in Pharaoh's palace as a prince."

"For heaven's sake, Effie," her mother scolded. "Come down to earth. It's almost time for lunch and then you'll have to be going to look after the baby."

The afternoon wore by slowly, too slowly to suit the fifteen-year-old baby-sitter. The more Effie tried to humor the infant, the louder the baby cried. "Brother, if there was a river close by, and I had a little basket, I know exactly what I'd do with you," she said. But even that threat failed to faze the noisy baby. In desperation she picked him up in her arms, and went out into the yard. "Maybe the house is too stuffy for you," she said, as she walked slowly around the yard, admiring the trees and listening to the birds chirping gaily in the treetops.

To her surprise, the baby gradually quieted down. When she spied the hammock swinging between two large oaks in the back yard, she had a sudden inspiration. Placing the infant tenderly in the middle of the hammock, she began to rock him back and forth with gentle motions. Soon, to her surprise, he was fast asleep. Afraid she would awaken him if she stopped rocking him back and forth, Effie stood faithfully by for the next hour. When she saw the breeze stirring the limbs in the top of the tree, she said to herself, "Wouldn't it be wonderful if there was a hammock way up there in the top of the tree. You wouldn't have to rock the baby back and forth because the wind would do that all by itself. But if the bough should break—well, that's a different matter."

When she saw the little lad stirring in his slumber, she began to hum softly to him and soon he was sound asleep once more. And just as soon, out of the blue, she found herself singing a song about a baby being rocked to sleep in a cradle in the top of the tree. The melody was all her very own, for all she knew, because it did not sound like anything she had ever heard. Even the lines were original, because they began with these words:

"Rock-a-bye baby, on the tree top, When the wind blows the cradle will rock."

When the infant's mother returned that memorable afternoon in 1887, Effie turned over the child to her care and went back to her own home down the street. Enroute, she scribbled the words of her lullaby on a page in a memorandum book. When she got home, she jotted down the music, and almost forgot all about it. The following Christmas, someone presented her with a banjo. She began to take lessons, and one afternoon she sang the new song for her teacher, asking him to show her how to play it on the banjo. Her teacher liked the new lullaby and sent her to a Boston music publisher, C. D. Blake, who was equally enthusiastic about it. But Effie Crockett had her doubts. She decided not to take any chances with her family name and reputation so she persuaded Mr. Blake to publish the song as a composition of Effie Canning. "I liked the name Canning," she explained later, "so I asked Mr. Blake to use it. I wasn't much impressed with the song, and didn't want it traced to me if it didn't fare well," she added.

Its success was assured after it was used in one scene in Denman Thompson's play "Tho Old Homestead." During the first few months after it was sung there, sales amounted to more than $20,000, and before Mr. Blake died, over 300,000 copies had been sold. Copyright mixups resulted in prolonged litigation which was never satisfactorily settled in the opinion of all parties concerned.

Effie Crockett married Harry G. Carlton, a character actor with David Belasco for sixteen years prior to his death in 1922. Ironically, they had no children of their own. She enjoyed a wonderful reputation as an actress, playing in Charles Frohman's production of "Oliver Twist," travelling for some years with her own repertory company and boasting a year's service as William Gilette's leading lady.

Before her death several years ago her later years were spent in a homey apartment not far from Boston's Symphony Hall.

Just as it was left to bachelor Isaac Watts to write the children's hymn, "Hush, my dear, lie still and slumber, Holy angels guard thy bed," so it was left to a baby-sitter who never had any children of her own to write the lullaby with which millions of mothers have sung and will forever continue to sing their own babies to sleep.

19.

SILVER THREADS AMONG THE GOLD

All his life Hart Pease Danks looked for the tide on which his ship would come sailing in. But he little dreamed that with the ebbing of the same tide, he would lose all that life held dear.

When he was twenty-four, this native of Connecticut married a Cleveland girl, Hattie R. Colahan, on January 25, 1858. "I feel like the psalmist," he said after the wedding. "My cup runneth over." Added happiness came to the couple with the birth of two lovely daughters and a son. The family left Chicago in 1864 and moved to New York City. Giving up his work as a successful builder, Danks devoted himself exclusively to music, serving as choir director in various churches and conducting musical societies and choral clubs on the side.

Taking a cue from Stephen Foster, he began composing sentimental songs about the south. But his best one, "De Cabin on de Mississippi Shore" lacked the emotional appeal of "Old Black Joe" and the catchiness of "Oh Susanna." However, he was more successful with his gospel songs. When he found a poem by John Clements based on the vision of "the city that lieth four-square" from Revelation 21:16, he promptly set it to music for a male quartet with which he sang. The lustre of this song, which became an immediate favorite in Churches and Sunday Schools, has not been dimmed with the passing of time. The first stanza contained these lines:

"In the land of fadeless day Lies the city four-square;
It shall never pass away, And there is no night there."

But his lucky day came when he picked up a Wisconsin farm journal and began browsing through its pages. Suddenly his eye fell upon a delightful little poem. "That's good," he said. "I'd like to set it to music for the quartet." Looking at the bottom of the page he noted that the poem was from the pen of the editor of the paper, Eben Eugene Rexford. Danks promptly sent a letter to him. "Dear Mr. Rexford," he wrote, "I came across a lovely little poem you wrote in a Wisconsin farm journal recently. It caught my fancy and I would like to have your permission to set it to music for a male quartet with which I sing here in New York. If you will be so kind as to grant me this favor, I will be glad to pay you $3 for all rights to your stanzas."

When he passed the good news on to the other three singers, the tenor asked, "What did he say, Hart? Can you use the poem?"

"Use it?" Danks replied. "He wrote me that he was so glad to know that somebody wanted one of his poems that, in addition to the one I saw in that magazine, he was giving me permission to compose tunes for a whole batch of original poems he promised to send me as soon as possible."

"Well, this may be your big chance, Hart," the baritone added. "Read them over carefully and don't let any gem slip through your fingers."

"Don't worry," the composer replied. "I'll keep my eyes and ears open." A few nights later, after the other men had gone home following another hour of rehearsing, Danks sat down a bit wearily and began to read through several poems which Eben Rexford had sent him. Mrs. Danks was sitting in an easy chair at the other end of the room, gathering up the loose ends of the day before retiring. Occasionally her husband would glance over, look at her, read another poem and then look over at her again. She was darning a pair of socks when he said, "Honey, listen to this poem that Mr. Rexford wrote. It fits us perfectly."

"What is it, dear?" she asked.

"A poem that could have been written for us. Listen." Referring to a piece of paper in his hand, he began to read aloud, slowly and with deep emotion. As he read, Mrs. Danks dropped her sewing into her lap, looked up at him lovingly and nodded in approval, because he was reading these lines:

Darling, I am growing old, Silver threads among the gold;
Shine upon my brow today, Life is fading fast away.
But, my darling, you will be, Always young and fair to me;
Yes, my darling, you will be, Always young and fair to me.

When he finished the third stanza, she said, "It's lovely, Hart; perfectly lovely. If ever a poet had us in mind, it was Mr. Rexford when he wrote those beautiful lines." Danks walked over to her side, put his arm about her tenderly. "We *are* growing old, darling, but our love is ageless. To me you will always be as radiant and as charming as you were the day we were married." He kissed her affectionately, and then went over to the piano at the other end of the room. As she sat there and listened attentively, thirty-nine-year-old Hart P. Danks sat at the keyboard. Before he retired that night, he had composed the music for his most popular song. "Our ship has already come in, Hart," she reminded him as they went upstairs to prepare for bed. "And instead of being laden down with pirate gold and treasure from the Spanish Main, it holds a cargo of love more valuable than gold and devotion more precious than any other treasure."

The poem by Eben Rexford (1848-1916) set to music by Hart P. Danks became an immediate success. During the next few years over two million copies were sold. But, as the money poured in, love flew out, and, after forty years of marriage, Hart and Hattie Danks broke up and went their separate ways, in 1898. Danks moved from New York to Philadelphia in 1903, living in a plain furnished room at 1210 Race Street. By that time he had composed more than twelve hundred tunes for hymns and sentimental songs. Some of his music was good enough to be included in Bradbury's "Jubilee Collection" while several of his anthems became standard selections for many Church choirs.

Thirty years after he had composed his most famous melody, his landlady, Mrs. Maud Hartman, found sixty-nine-year-old Mr. Danks on his knees, cold and still in death. It was November 20, 1903. When his body was moved, lying on his cot was a piece of music entitled, "Silver Threads Among the Gold." And on this piece of music which had brought him fame and fortune, the composer had scribbled his own epitaph with the stub of a pencil which he still clutched in his cold and lifeless fingers, "It's hard to grow old alone——." His widow died in Brooklyn twenty years later. Possibly in the other world, in the words of his best-known gospel song, "God shall wipe away all tears," and the night of their earthly disappointment shall give way to the radiant dawn of an undying love.

20.

SWEET ADELINE

Australian soprano, Nellie Melba, had a favorite dessert. It consisted of a half a peach inverted on a piece of cake, surrounded by whipped cream. Today it is familiarly known as "Peach Melba." Italy's equally renowned soprano, Luise Tetrazzini, preferred entrees to desserts and "Chicken Tetrazzini" is still a gourmet's delight. But Spanish-born soprano, Adelina Patti, whose remarkable operatic career spanned half a century, little dreamed that she would be the inspiration for one of the most popular convivial ballads ever written. She wouldn't have been, though, if the lyrist could have dug another name to rhyme with "pine."

A piano-playing pugilist named Harry Armstrong tried his hand at song writing and, when a mere lad of seventeen, dashed off a ditty which he called "My Old New England Home." Somehow or other it failed to catch on. The music was sweet and harmonious and the words contained the usual sentimental slush that was the rage at the turn of the century. But the combination of the two left the publishers cold. The boxer was smart, though, and quit the ring before becoming too punch-drunk to continue plunking out his songs and plugging them before the publishers as well as the crowds that hung around the corner taverns. In New York City he struck up an acquaintance with Jimmy Walker, who was to become the nation's Number One Mayor later on.

"Jimmy," the composer said one day, "I want you to listen to a piece of music I wrote back in '96. I think it's got something."

"All right, Harry," the future politician replied. "Let's have it." Since the two men had already collaborated on a fairly suc-

86

cessful song, "Goodbye Eyes of Blue," each respected the judgment of the other. Armstrong played over his music but Jimmy couldn't come up with the right combination of words. On second thought he said, "I know just the man for you, Harry. He is Richard Gerard Husch. But he prefers to swap his middle and last names and be known as Richard H. Gerard."

"I've heard of him," Armstrong interrupted. "Is he that good?"

"Give him a try," Walker insisted. "You can't lose."

Encouraged by Walker, Armstrong looked up Gerard and located him in a Twenty-eighth Street bar, and soon the poet was as enthusiastic about the new song's possibilities as the composer. In his Greenwich Village room he hummed over the music, trying to devise just the right formula to put it over. "I'll discard this New England home approach," he told his friend later, "and work on an entirely different angle."

"It's all right with me. You know the music, so dream up the words and our troubles will be over," Armstrong added.

The following day Gerard had a sudden inspiration. "That's it," he said to himself. "I'll start with 'Sweet Rosalie.'" When he told Armstrong, the musician admitted that the new second line "For you I pine" didn't rhyme with "Sweet Rosalie," but that he liked the second line better than the first. The two men finally decided to find a name that would rhyme with "pine." They tried them all from Evelyn to Jacqueline, and from Columbine to Clementine, but none of them 'clicked.'

"Think it over, Richard," the composer suggested. "It'll come to you when you least expect it." And he was right. While Gerard was walking home that night, he saw a series of large colorful billboard posters announcing a forthcoming concert by the world famous prima donna, Adelina Patti. He stopped in his tracks. "That's it," he shouted. "Adeline!" And "Adeline" it was. He would never again stumble upon such a lucky break; and a more fortunate wedding of words and music would never again be his.

But even then the publishers were not too enthusiastic and the song gathered dust and cobwebs for several years. Finally in 1903 a well-known quartet that went by the name of "The Quaker City Four" dusted it off and discovered to everyone's amazement that it was an instantaneous hit; in fact, it was almost a sensation!

Unfortunately it soon left the concert stage and the theatre and was relegated to the barber shop and barroom. The song deserved a better fate, but the makeshift quartets that could only harmonize when they "had a few under their belts" made "Sweet Adeline" their very own. And, as the song had been written bar by bar, so it spread from bar to bar as well as from barber shop to barber shop until it became the most popular song of joyful conviviality the last century produced. Adelina deserved a better break too, but had she to choose between a dessert or an entree or a song, undoubtedly she would have chosen the latter.

Lyrist Gerard never "hit the jackpot" again. Settling down as foreman of the application file bureau of the money order division at Manhattan's General Post Office, he plugged away at his job until his retirement at seventy in 1946. During that time he dashed off about two-hundred-fifty more poems, but none of them equal to his one great hit, "Sweet Adeline." Few people knew that the "friendly, stocky man with a shiny bald head, bending over a desk figuring accounts in the Post Office" was the author of this famous ballad. He explained his retirement to his friends by saying, "I want to knock off a few hits." But before he got around to it, he dropped dead of a heart attack on a Manhattan street just two years later, dying at seventy-two.

While the collaborators made a small fortune from their "hit," their deepest satisfaction must have come from the knowledge that they had actually produced a song that had become so familiar that the names of the author and composer had almost been forgotten. To be remembered by being forgotten is an honor accorded to very few!

21.

THE BATTLE CRY OF FREEDOM

"I'm sorry, but there hasn't been a dramatic episode behind any of my songs," George Frederick Root said to his guests. "I know this will come as a disappointment to you, but it's the truth."

One of the high school girls asked, "Then you just sat down at the piano and wrote them? Is that it?"

"That's about it, young lady," the famed composer replied.

"Boy, what a let down," one of the boys added. "And here I was, all set for a thrilling story."

"I'm sorry to let you down, young man," Mr. Root said, "but facts are facts whether they fit into your theories or not."

The second lad broke into the conversation. "What gave us the idea, Mr. Root, was a story we heard last week about the writing of the Civil War song 'We are coming, Father Abraham.' I read somewhere that during the Seven Days Battles on the outskirts of Richmond, June 25 to July 1, 1862, General McClellan was pushed back by General Lee and the Federal Army lost many men. In fact the casualties were so heavy that President Lincoln issued a proclamation calling for at least three hundred thousand new soldiers right away, to rebuild the Army of the Potomac. One of those who was deeply impressed by the President's plea was Mr. James Sloan Gibbons, a banker, a strong abolitionist and a song-writer who lived in Wilmington, Delaware. As he listened to the tramping feet of the new recruits marching down the streets of his city, he caught the rhythm of their steady beat and sat down and wrote the song 'We are coming, Father Abraham, three hundred thousand more.' The words were first published in the July 16, 1862 issue of the New York Evening Post."

"So we wondered," one of the girls added, "if you had had similar experiences in writing your popular war songs."

"I wish I had had some of those experiences, young lady," the elderly musician continued, "but my songs didn't arise from such dramatic episodes. You may be interested, though, in knowing that I, too, was moved by Lincoln's request for new recruits. I, too, felt that someone should set his call to music. So, not knowing that Gibbons was doing the very thing in Delaware, I sat down at my piano and wrote 'The Battle Cry of Freedom.' It was sung for the first time by the well-known Lubard Brothers in a war rally in Chicago, and, to my great surprise, was an immediate hit. A few days later the Hutchinson family used it in another rally in New York City, at Union Square, and its popularity in the east dates from that occasion. But I must confess that when I wrote it, I had no idea that I was writing a successful song or one that would catch on so quickly."

"Mr. Root," one of the girls asked, "did you ever write a song that you wished later you hadn't written?"

"During the heat of war time," the aged author confessed, "it is easy to write songs condemning all the enemy and sending him to perdition, while holding up our own side as perfectly righteous and honest and pure in every act as well as motive. That seems to be a natural tendency. But when the wars are over, we learn that the enemy had men as brave, as sincere and as courageous as our own. And then we wish we had not written so dogmatically about our virtues and their vices."

"Have you written any songs about the tragedy of war?" another youth asked.

Mr. Root sat deep in thought for a few moments and then said, "Yes, young man, I have. 'Tramp, Tramp, Tramp the boys are marching' is just such a song. It leaves out the praise and heroics and shallow patriotism and reminds us that war is a dirty, bloody mess that ought never to have been. And there is my song about a family gathering around the table after a son has been lost in battle. It is called 'The Vacant Chair' and begins, 'We shall meet but we will miss him, There will be one vacant chair.' "

"I remember that one, Mr. Root," one girl remarked. "It's different from the others because it is sad."

"You may be interested in knowing that my songs tell the story of war from beginning to end, " Mr. Root continued. "In '61, I wrote 'The battle cry of freedom' to rouse the men to action. Then in '63 I composed 'Just before the battle, mother' and in '64, the experiences of a prisoner of war in 'Tramp tramp tramp the boys are marching' and finally the loss of life in 'The vacant chair.' That's the way it usually goes: enlistment, battle, imprisonment, death, and it is a terrible story to have to extol in song, isn't it?"

"But you have written other songs that we sing in Sunday School and Church, haven't you, Mr. Root?" one of the boys asked. "I think I've seen your name in several of our hymnals and song books."

"Yes, young man, you are right," the elderly musician replied. "I am prouder of those tunes than of anything else I have been privileged to compose."

"Our glee club at school sings one of your songs, 'There's music in the air.' In fact, it's one of our favorites," the youth continued.

"Which tunes are *your* favorites, Mr. Root?" one of the girls asked.

The older man thought for a moment and then answered, "I like the tune which I named 'Varina.' In most hymnals it is used with the words of Isaac Watts, 'There is a land of pure delight Where saints immortal reign.' My tune 'Ellon' is also one I am pleased with. It is not as popular as 'Varina' but recently I discovered that a new hymn for children, 'The wise may bring their learning' was being sung to my music. And don't forget the other children's hymn, 'Precious Jewels.' "

91

"We used to sing that in the junior choir," one of the girls added. "It's a beautiful song."

"It isn't often that a successful hymn writer composes equally successful popular and patriotic songs, is it?" one youth asked.

"It may seem a rather rare combination," Mr. Root replied, "but I hope my hymn tunes and religious songs live long after my patriotic airs have been forgotten."

Root's "Memoirs" were published in Cincinnati in 1891, just four years before his death which occurred during his seventy-fifth year at Bailey's Island, Maine, August 6, 1895. Time alone will tell whether his war songs or his religious music will live longest in the hearts of the American people.

22.

THE BATTLE HYMN OF THE REPUBLIC

William Steffe turned to the director. "Where are the books?" he asked. The director looked a bit puzzled. "What books, Mr. Steffe?" "The song books," Steffe replied. "Oh," the director said as he smiled. "We don't have any song books." "No books? Why not? I've come all the way from Richmond to lead the singing in this camp meeting and now I find you haven't any song books," the young song-leader continued.

"Well, Mr. Steffe," the director explained, "it's this way. The folks who can read can't sing and those who can sing can't read." Steffe and his friends laughed. "What am I supposed to do, then?" he inquired. "Make up your own songs," the director suggested. "Are you serious?" Steffe asked. "Yes," the director replied. "If we don't have any song books and you're the song-leader for the camp meeting, there's nothing else to do but write your own songs."

With that, the director turned and left the brush arbor auditorium, leaving the puzzled song-leader more perplexed than ever. When Steffe accepted the invitation to direct the music that summer in 1852, he thought his duties would consist of leading the congregational singing at all public gatherings, present sacred solos and getting up an occasional quartet or choir special for some of the meetings. As for writing his own songs, that was out of the question.

Steffe turned to one of his associates. "What do we do now?" he asked. "Do what the man says, William," his friend replied. "Write your own songs." "About what?" the young Richmonder asked. "About things that folks who go to Georgia camp meetings agree on. Not about anything controversial like

93

slavery or the industrial north trying to put the squeeze on the agricultural south, or Washington politics."

"Well," the young Virginian continued, "what do camp meeting folks agree on that we can sing about? What to eat or what to drink or what to wear?"

"No," his friend suggested. "They are Christians and active Church members for the most part."

"And what do most Christians agree on?" Steffe broke in. "They all had a mother. You can't argue that point. And they all hope to get to heaven when they die; that's painfully obvious, or else they wouldn't be here."

His friend added, "So write a song about mother or about heaven."

"To what tune?" asked Steffe.

"Make up your own tune," his friend replied. "And take a cue from the Negro spirituals. Use the same music for the verse as for the chorus, only change the words. And use a lot of repetition, saying the same phrase over and over again. If you do that, you're made, William."

"I know," William replied, "and if I don't, I'm busted. That's what is worrying me." One of the boys picked up his guitar and strummed a few chords. Steffe borrowed it immediately. "Let me try my hand at this," he said. "Maybe we can write that new song after all." He picked out a few chords as the others gathered around. "As for the words, we'll write our song like the spirituals, using the same tune for the chorus as for the verse. Now let's get started." After a few suggestive themes and titles, Steffe looked up and said, "I think I have it, fellows."

"What is it?" they asked eagerly.

"We'll write a song about heaven and make it in the form of a question. Here's the first verse: Say brothers, will you meet us? Say brothers, will you meet us? Say brothers, will you meet us, On Canaan's happy shore?"

"Good, but what about the chorus?" a friend asked.

"We'll use the same music but we'll use these words: Glory, glory hallelujah; Glory, glory hallelujah; Glory, glory hallelujah,

94

Forever evermore." "Excellent," the others remarked, applauding. "That song's a natural," someone else added, "because you can sing, Say sisters will you meet us; Say uncle will you meet us, and on and on as long as you want to." Steffe said, "And if the bishop gets mired down on his way from Charleston, we can sing about the deacons, and stewards and aunts and cousins until he gets here for his sermon. Then we'll add a word of affirmation, by singing, 'By the grace of God we'll meet you' and close with 'Jesus lives and reigns forever On Canaan's happy shore.' "

The new song was an immediate success, especially the rousing chorus that began "Glory glory hallelujah!" Soon everyone in and around the site of the camp meeting was singing it to beat the band, and it wasn't long before travellers going north and south picked up the strains and carried them home to the far expanses of the growing republic. "It's a natural," they said; and it was.

After John Brown's raid on the arsenal at Harper's Ferry, Virginia, and his death in 1859, his followers and sympathizers picked up the strains of Steffe's hymn and told the world that while "John Brown's body lies a-mouldering in the grave, His soul goes marching on." And many who never heard of "Say brothers will you meet us" sang the new song as if it were an original patriotic air inspired by the abortive effort to release the slaves on the part of the fanatical mid-western apostle of freedom.

When the Civil War broke out, the Twelfth Massachusetts Regiment, commanded by Colonel Fletcher Webster, was ordered from Boston to Washington for the defense of the capital. Enroute they sang the new song and people took up the strains with wild enthusiasm, thinking it was a new marching hymn for the Union in the fight against the rebelling, seceding Confederates. So "Glory glory hallelujah" came to Washington, D.C., where forty-two-year-old Julia Ward Howe, wife of a distinguished physician connected with the government's Sanitary Commission, heard it for the first time in November, 1861. She felt the emotional impact of the music, but realized that

95

the stanzas were totally inadequate for a lasting hymn. Her middle-aged pastor, Rev. James Freeman Clarke, urged her to write some original stanzas to be sung to that popular tune, hinting that her poem could well be a battle hymn for the Republic. Late that November night, from their room in the Willard Hotel, Mrs. Howe could see the watch fires of a hundred circling camps, and hear the trumpet that would never sound retreat. With the strains of the familiar melody now beating in her heart, she sat down and began to write as stirring a poem as has ever come from feminine fingers, and as militant a hymn as has ever been composed by one who had never shouldered a musket or obeyed a military order:

Mine eyes have seen the glory of the coming of the Lord,
He is trampling out the vintage where the grapes of wrath are
    stored;
He hath loosed the fateful lightning of His terrible swift sword,
His truth is marching on.

The five stanzas were first published in the Atlantic Monthly, February 1862, and the hymn was accepted immediately as a battle song for the Republic during the remaining years of the tragic War Between the States. Little did the Yankees dream, as they invaded the southern states singing their new battle hymn, that it was in reality the composition of a Richmonder for a Georgia camp meeting. Strangely enough, neither did the southerners dream, as they fought to repulse the invader singing their own marching song, "Dixie," that it had been written and composed by an Ohio boy in New York City several years earlier.

But that is another story!

23.

THE END OF A PERFECT DAY

The life of Carrie Jacobs Bond was fraught with tragedy. Hardly would she get over one sorrow before another was knocking at her door. Born in Janesville, Wisconsin in 1862, she early showed an unusual interest in music and painting. During her childhood, spent on the fifteen-acre farm that belonged to her father, she soon learned to play the piano by ear. With uncanny talent, she could listen to a selection and play it on the piano with unerring accuracy.

But tragedy haunted the shadows of her life, lurking behind the curtain of every success. Shortly after her seventh birthday, she ran into a hired girl who was carrying a tub of scalding hot water. She carried the mark of those burns on her body the rest of her life. The shock to her nervous system was one from which she never fully recovered. On top of that, her doctor father, who had encouraged his talented daughter to develop her musical talent, died that same year.

Then came her first marriage, at eighteen, to E. J. Smith. Some years later, after the birth of a son, they were divorced. But providence showed His smiling face behind the darkening clouds, and at twenty-five she fell in love with a childhood sweetheart, Dr. Frank Lewis Bond, and they were married. He, like her gifted father, recognized the talents hidden away in the heart of the young woman, and did his best to encourage her. "Dr. Bond thought I could write songs," she told a friend. "I played for him as I could never play for anyone else. We had a castle in the air and there was music in every room."

The depth of his love for her and her love for him tapped resources deep inside her soul that she had not known existed and there flowed out a flood of music such as she had never produced before. But their happiness was almost too good to be true, and when tragedy struck this time, it struck with a double blow. The doctor, starting out on a round of visits to some of his patients one cold wintry night, slipped and fell. Despite the loving and tender care she lavished upon him, he died within a week.

When she began settling up his affairs, word came that a mining company in which most of his capital was invested, had been declared bankrupt. So, at thirty-two, when most people dream of settling down, Carrie Jacobs Bond, widowed for the second time, with a nine-year-old son to provide for, had to start all over again. When the debts were finally paid off, she was left with a little insurance money, the gift of music and a broken heart that she felt would never sing again.

Looking back on the days of her poverty she was to say, when future years had seen her gain the reputation and security she well deserved, "I am glad I have been poor, for being poor makes one more human. But for poverty I may never have been able to write the songs which have brought success." With her piano as her most valued possession, she and her son moved to Chicago, living in a few rooms over a restaurant. She secured odd jobs, renting rooms, painting china and giving informal concerts to publicize the songs she had begun to write. But success eluded her, and for some years she and her boy ate sparingly and wore whatever her paltry income could provide.

When music publishers rejected her songs, she began printing them herself, her first publishing house being the hall bedroom of her apartment. But her venture into the publishing field only left her more deeply in debt than ever before. So she borrowed money and moved her 'Bond Shop' into the dining room. When someone asked her years later, "Why didn't you give up?" she replied, "It never occurred to me." With the skills developed in china-painting, she decorated the covers of the first copies of her songs with wreaths of wild roses. Her son peddled the songs to several Chicago stores on his bicycle, but most of the managers said politely, "Sorry; not interested." So she decided to publicize them herself by giving concerts and appearing in theatres and other public places. It was hard at first, and she suffered the humiliations many other artists endured before she gained the confidence and charm that enabled her to put her songs over before different groups of people. When even that failed to convince the publishers that her music was eminently worth while, she decided upon the boldest stroke of all, and took her songs with her to the dressing room of the prima donna of the Boston Opera Company, Jessie Bartlett Davis. The famous singer was enchanted with seven songs which Mrs. Bond played and sang that fateful afternoon. "You must have them published at once and I will sing them," she said enthusiastically. When the composer explained that she did not have that kind of money, Mrs. Davis wrote out her own personal check to cover the balance due, and "Seven Songs" by Carrie Jacobs Bond was published. The slender little volume contained these musical gems, "I love you truly," written to commemorate the great love of her life, and "Just A-Wearyin' for You," from the pen of a noted American statesman, for which she composed her lilting melody. The songs soon became part of the repertoire of other established artists and in a short time more than a million copies were sold.

But the spectre of sorrow haunted even her hours of success. Early in 1910 she wrote the words of her most popular song after a drive up Mount Ribidoux, near Riverside, California, to watch the gorgeous sunset. Three months later, during a night drive through the Mohave Desert, she composed the music and gave to the world one of its perennial favorites, "The end of a perfect day." When she heard the soldiers singing this song during the first World War, she said, "I am glad I wrote heart songs instead of becoming a great musician."

Her son, the constant companion and co-worker of her lean years as well as her successful years, suffered a severe illness in 1932. In a fit of depression following the period of sickness he took his own life. His mother, now accustomed to walking hand-in-hand with sorrow, continued to write her songs out of the dreams of a love that almost died a-borning, and a series of heartaches that brought her more than her share of pain.

On her eightieth birthday in 1942 she said, "I try to find the peace and happiness which the world of today seems to have lost." Asked about modern music, from swing to bop, she commented, "I prefer the music that touches closer to the heart." That she had made her contribution to the heart music of America, no one will deny. Its outreach is in direct proportion to the depths of agony out of which it sprung, and its inspiration is a fitting tribute to the indomitable spirit of a very remarkable woman. The five million people who have bought copies of "The end of a perfect day" will say "Amen!"

24.

THE KASHMIRI SONG

Love is still the greatest theme in the world, but whether its joys or its sorrows evoke the deepest emotions or stir the profoundest feelings has never been determined. But unrequited love still haunts the heart of the poet with a sadness that is enjoyable at the same time that it seems most unbearable, until, to some, the agony of losing becomes a more pleasurable experience than the joy of possessing. In broken hearts, pain can actually become a kind of distorted pleasure, until one prefers to remain alone with the heartache of an old love than try to erase its scars with the anticipated thrills of a new love.

Such emotions were stirring in the heart of the mountain girl who was about to lose her beloved. The crying of the night wind was but a tangible expression of the wailing within her heart at the thought of his going, while the very flowers that grew in wild profusion down in the valley bespoke the tenderness in which she held his devotion. But he was going, and with him, she felt, was going whatever happiness earth could afford or heaven could promise.

"If I could only see him again," she cried. "If I could only see him, my heart would not throb with such fierceness and intensity, and this emptiness within my soul, this aching void, would not seem so deep and bottomless."

But the road he was to travel was on the far side of the range, and he had already said his last goodbye and planted upon her lips the kiss that was to be the benediction to their romance. Struggling to hold back the tears, she cried, "Build me a castle, forty feet high, So I can see him as he rides by."

Those who lived out their days in the dull routine of work and sleep could never know what was going on within her heart. To most of them, love was a one-syllable word in the dictionary to be used at weddings as a matter of ceremony and then relegated to the intimacies of a mother's relationships to her babies, or to the first flush of an adolescent awakening. But she knew it was both the beginning and the end of life, without which there was no reason for further existence, and with which she could brave the very gates of hell. Out of her pain came the haunting strains of the American folk song, "Down in the valley," whose mood and message only those who have loved deeply can sense and appreciate.

But the mountain lass was not alone in her experience. It had been shared by many before her coming and would be the common lot of others after she had passed from this mortal scene.

In far off India, the land of romance and enchantment, Adela Florence Cory, young, charming and very beautiful, married General Malcolm Nicholson who was not only twenty-five years her senior but a typical stern, dignified, unexpressive, humorless professional military man who looked with disdain upon the carefree, spontaneous and effervescent soul of the stunning girl he had been privileged to marry. So, beneath the shadows of a distant temple, against the exotic background of weird music and warm nights, in the desperate search for something to give her life meaning and purpose, she gave her heart to another. But their romance was doomed to failure almost before it began, because she fell in love with a handsome son of an Indian Rajah. To ease the anguish within her soul, she poured out her agony in a series of delicate and beautiful poems. When her lover was given an ultimatum by his father, they met for the last time, pledged their love until eternity, kissed each other passionately, and then parted forever. "Ah," she wrote, "I would rather have his hands at my throat crushing out life than waving me farewell. They led me far on rapture's roadway. Will they lead another until she, too, agonizes in farewell?"

Her poems were later published under the pen name of Laurence Hope, and England applauded the artistry of the verses, little dreaming of the pain in which they had been conceived and the suffering which served as their accompaniment. One of these poems has outlived the ill-fated romance which inspired the tender little volume, and goes down in anthologies and on concert programs as "The Kashmiri Song," by Laurence Hope, but its haunting lines are permeated with heartache and pain, weariness and despair and a question which asks God why He would doom two of his children, who were so magically and providentially drawn together, to eternal separation. Almost the poems ask whether great loves ever exist in real life or only in books conceived in the fertile or thwarted imaginations of gifted novelists and story-tellers.

A minister was dying in the great city of Chicago in November, 1896. Just a few days earlier he had written to a friend in Zanesville, Ohio, the site of his first pastorate, these tragic lines, "I doubt if all the dark lines are erased from my heart yet."

The pastor was Rev. H. D. L. Webster, the story of whose unrequited love is recorded in his original poem, "Lorena." The family of the girl he loved refused to permit her to marry "a poor country preacher" and the couple had reluctantly broken off their engagement. "Time will heal our wounds," she had told him, only to hear him reply, "How can time heal a love that is timeless? Or how can distance erase a love that you carry down inside your soul?" But he had gone his way and she hers. And she had married a brilliant young attorney, William W. Johnson, and settled down in Ironton, Lawrence County, Ohio. He proved a remarkably successful lawyer, soon being appointed a Judge in his county. Webster, meanwhile, settled down in Wisconsin, gradually making a name for himself as a poet and journalist. He always felt that she continued to love him as he continued to love her, time and space notwithstanding, and when "Lorena" brought forth no response on her part, he penned a sequel in which he expressed the hope that he would be joined to his Lorena, if not here, then surely in the hereafter. He referred to himself in the second poem as Paul Vane, and it was under that name that the stanzas were published, set to music and sung throughout the country. Lorena's husband died at the height of his influence in 1887, and she returned to the scenes of her childhood at Zanesville, passing her last years there practically alone, since most of her relatives had preceded her into the great beyond. She had been a "faithful helpmate" to Judge Johnson, sharing his high honors "with becoming dignity," but one wonders whether he ever tapped the depths of her heart and drew from her soul the kind of love that could have been hers had Lorena and Paul Vane married.

Such is the story of the mountain maiden who gave up her beloved, the General's wife who was torn from her Indian lover and the heart-broken minister who was separated from his Lorena, and one wonders whether those tragedies were of God or of His adversary, the Devil!

25.

THE LOST CHORD

The doctor shook his head. "I'm sorry, Mr. Sullivan," he said.

"Then there is no hope for my brother's life?" Arthur Sullivan asked, fearfully.

"None," the physician replied. "The case is now in the hands of God. Medical science has done all that is humanly possible. If he lives, it will be a miracle."

Arthur Sullivan sat down in a chair at the bedside of his dying brother. "Nothing short of a miracle," he said, repeating the words the doctor had just uttered. "Then I'll pray for a miracle, Doctor. He's my favorite brother. We've been devoted to each other from earliest boyhood," the distraught musician continued. "And if it's a miracle you need, we'll ask the Almighty to intervene."

"I'll be back later this evening," the doctor said as he put on his coat. "If he passes before then, please let me know."

The composer arose. "I will, Doctor. And thank you for your patience and understanding during these very trying days," he said, as he walked with him toward the door. "It hasn't been easy. You know that."

"I know it, Arthur," the physician replied. "But his condition is so bad that death would be a blessing. It would release your brother from the prison-house of a worn-out body into the freedom of the love of God. So, when you are praying for him, say a prayer for yourself, that you may be able to endure his death as a Christian should."

After the doctor had gone, Arthur Sullivan resumed his place at his brother's bedside. During the next few hours he busied himself trying to break the fever that seemed to be burning the dying man with unrelenting fury. But the more he tried to do, the less capable he felt, until, finally, in disgust as well as despair, he shoved all the medicines aside and knelt in prayer near the foot of the bed. After a few minutes he rose wearily to his feet, straightened the sheets on the bed, and went into the adjoining room to try to find solace at his beloved piano. Melodies from his successful light opera "Trial by Jury," composed two years before, in 1875, were to no avail at a time like this. So he played over some of the hymn tunes he had written, trying to draw spiritual succor from the lines and stanzas which had become so precious to him. Going from one tune to another, he played the tunes Homeland (The Homeland, O the Homeland, his first hymn tune, composed in 1867), St. Gertrude (Onward Christian Soldiers, 1871), St. Kevin (Come Ye Faithful, Raise the Strain, 1872), St. Edmund (Draw Thou My Soul O Christ, 1872), Courage, Brother (Courage Brother, Do Not Stumble, 1872), Angel Voices (Angel Voices Ever Singing, 1872), Samuel (Hushed Was the Evening Hymn, 1874), St. Theresa (Brightly Gleams Our Banner, 1874), Constance (I've Found a Friend, 1875), until the tension within his soul began to give way to a calm serenity coupled with the assurance of God's abiding presence.

"I know his death is inevitable," he said to himself, "and I want to prepare myself for it. I don't want to be rebellious, as if God were trying to punish me, but grateful that God gives to his beloved the gift of death." He rose, walked into the sickroom again, picked up a book from a nearby table and began browsing through its pages to pass the long sleepless hours away. He glanced at the title page after reading a few selections, and noticed that the book was entitled "Legends and Lyrics, a Book of Verses" by Adelaide Anne Procter, published in 1858. "Nineteen years ago," he said, "and it is more popular now than the year she published it."

He dropped the volume in his lap and began to reminisce about the life of this unusual and talented woman. He recalled the oft-told story of the day Charles Dickens had visited the

Procter home in London, and how, during the conversation that followed dinner, he spoke enthusiastically of the writings of one Mary Berwick which he had been publishing in "Household Words" for several years, and he even read to his hosts one or two of her poems. When the family burst into laughter, the distinguished novelist was flabbergasted, until Mr. Procter explained that the author was none other than his own daughter, "golden-tressed Adelaide." "Just as I published my first writings under the pseudonym 'Barry Cornwall,' so my daughter took the name 'Mary Berwick' lest you felt obligated to publish her contributions out of friendship for the family instead of judging them on their own merits," her father explained. With that, the famous English man of letters shared in the laughter which rang through the rafters of the London home.

Sullivan thought of the unselfish way in which the gifted poet had given herself to the care of the poor, until her own health broke under the strain. For fifteen months she had been confined to her bed, but remained always "cheerful and vivacious" to the very end.

Opening the book again, he read one of her autobiographical hymns, entitled "Through Peace to Light" which contained these lines:

I do not ask, O Lord, That life may be A pleasant road;
I do not ask that Thou wouldst take from me Aught of its load.
I do not ask my cross to understand, My way to see;
Better in darkness just to feel Thy hand, And follow Thee.

"Published at thirty-three; dead at thirty-nine," he said. "And here I am at thirty-five, wondering how I am going to take my brother's imminent death, and how I will confront life after he has gone." Soon he was reading another poem, "The Shadows of the Evening Hours," and was amazed at the spirit of acceptance and resignation which characterized Miss Procter during her fatal illness. A few pages further he began to read still another poetic gem from her fluent pen. But this time the words laid hold upon him with a grip that would not let go. It was the story she must have experienced in a great Church or dreamed of having happened while visiting one of England's noble cathedrals during or just after an organ recital. Yet how appropriate the words were right here and right now. For the poem began:

Seated one day at the organ, I was weary and ill at ease,
And my fingers wandered idly, Over the noisy keys;
I know not what I was playing, Nor what I was dreaming then,
Till I struck one chord of music Like the sound of a great Amen.

On and on he read, drinking in the words like a thirsty traveller gulping a glass of cold water, until he reached the grand climax:

It may be that Death's bright angel Will speak in that chord again,
It may be that only in heav'n, I shall hear that grand Amen.

Turning toward the bed, Arthur Sullivan said, "For you, my dear brother, for you I shall compose music for this poem that will sing its way into immortality!" And that fateful night in 1877, Sullivan, who was to become Sir Arthur (1842-1900) when knighted by the Queen in 1883, found both solace and strength in writing this musical epitaph for his beloved brother, and gave to the world one of its grandest affirmations of faith in the triumph of eternal life over the tragedy of death.

26.

THE MARSEILLAISE

Military men don't usually write military songs. They are generally so busy making, giving and carrying out orders that they have neither the time nor the talent necessary to produce a good song. A peace-loving Baptist preacher, Samuel Francis Smith, wrote our noblest patriotic poem, "America" in 1832, and another Baptist clergyman turned editor penned the most remarkable bit of patriotic prose in our nation's history. Rev. Francis Bellamy wrote "The Pledge of Allegiance to the Flag" in 1892. And a woman who never shouldered a musket dashed off one of the most militant poems ever written. Julia Ward Howe was the woman and her poem is known as "The battle hymn of the Republic."

But it does happen occasionally that a soldier rises to the occasion, this being the exception that proves the rule. So it was on that memorable night of April 24, 1792. A young officer in the French army, Rouget de Lisle, was something of a musician. While the military code could not compel him to write a song at the command of a superior officer, nevertheless etiquette and common sense would make him think twice before refusing a superior's request to that effect. So when an officer asked Infantry Captain de Lisle to write a new regimental song for the six hundred volunteers housed at Strasbourg, France under his command, young de Lisle wrote the words and music of "The Marseillaise" in a single night. He dedicated the song to Count Nikolaus Luckner, commander of the Luckner Hussars, who had come to the aid of King Louis XV of France in 1763 and who had remained to serve the Republic. The shifting fortunes of French politics are always a cross between quicksand and a quagmire, and the same Luckner who was heralded as a hero in 1792 was led to the guillotine in January of the next year. It was his great-grandson, Count Felix von Luckner, who evened the score. Known as the "Sea Wolf," he harried the convoys and sunk more than a half a million tons of allied shipping during the early years of the first World War.

The new song met with an enthusiastic response from the soldiers for whom it had been composed. But it was sung with even more intense fervor by troops from the seaport city of Marseille when they arrived in Paris and attacked the Tuileries on August 10, 1792. In honor of the way these soldiers sang the new song, it was named for the city in which they had been quartered, and the French national anthem to this day is called "The Marseillaise."

Nearly a hundred years later, two mild, peace-loving Frenchmen collaborated on another patriotic song, and, in 1885, turned out what they called "The Internationale." Poet Pottier and composer Degeyter little dreamed, as they heard Parisians singing the song in the streets and in the sidewalk cafes, that years later it would become the national anthem of Communist Russia.

Another officer who "hit the ball" with a stirring song at the right time was Lieutenant Edmund L. Gruber, of the United States Fifth Field Artillery, stationed in 1908 in the Philippine Islands. When the First and Fifth arrived to relieve the Second Battalion, someone suggested that a new song honoring the combined battalions was in order. Gruber, no relation to the Austrian organist who composed the music for "Silent Night," being the only musician in the crowd was unanimously elected. But since it is always easier ordered than produced, Gruber began to look around for an idea worth singing about. Some days later he was standing on top of a high hill watching a scouting party work its way through some rough inland country. When he heard officers in the distance urging their men and mounts along the upward trails into the hills, he became alarmed, thinking something was going wrong. A sergeant standing nearby said, "Don't worry, Lieutenant. They'll be all right if they keep 'em rolling." "That's it," shouted the future Major, and before nightfall he had composed "The Caisson Song" in which "the caissons keep rolling along." This song has become famous as the artilleryman's song of the United States Army.

The officer with a heart as well as a head was General Daniel Butterfield, who served with the Army of the Potomac during the Civil War. He had Oliver W. Norton as his brigade bugler. Following the brilliant defense of Richmond in July, 1862, when General Robert E. Lee had hurled back the superior forces of General McClellan's encircling army with tremendous casualties, the Federals retreated down the peninsula. The Seven Days Battles around Richmond had taken a terrific toll on both sides. Now the northern forces were waiting at Harrison's Landing on the James River, nursing their wounds and burying their dead. The General felt the atmosphere of gloom which permeated the camp and wanted to do something to calm the spirits of his men and encourage them at the same time. Being something of a musician and composer he felt moved that night to discard the usual 'Lights Out' bugle call and began humming over a new call to himself. In a short while he had figured out just what he wanted. Going over it with Bugler Norton, he perfected the new call and that very same night, over the stillness of the camp, the first plaintive notes of "Taps" sounded through a dark Virginia night. The effect was all that the General had desired. It caught the imaginations of the men and quieted them down. It seemed to be a rare combination of a summons to arms and a prayer for peace being blown at the same time by the same bugler. Soon thereafter, "Taps" was used throughout the entire Army of the Potomac, and later was substituted for the 'Lights Out' call in official Army regulations. So today, the blowing of "Taps" is accompanied with hushed reverence as it is sounded as a prayer at the close of the day and as a requiem at the close of a fighting man's life.

27

THE SIDEWALKS OF NEW YORK

If the good die young, song-writers must be a bad lot, because their record for longevity isn't too bad. While few popular song-writers have lived as long as hymn writer Fanny Crosby, who reached ninety-five, or the composer of numerous hymn and song tunes, George Stebbins, who celebrated his ninety-ninth birthday, several passed the mythical three-score-and-ten with flying colors.

Percy Wenrich, composer of "Put on your old gray bonnet," "Moonlight bay," and "When you wore a tulip" lived to be seventy-two before his death in 1952; Egbert Anson Van Alstyne, whose name will go down in musical history as long as people sing "In the shade of the old apple tree," "Pretty baby," and "Your eyes have told me so," died in 1951 at the age of seventy-three; and John Keirn Brennan, among whose successes are "Let the rest of the world go by" and "Little bit of heaven," reached his seventy-fourth birthday before he passed on in 1948. James Thornton, who composed "My sweetheart's the man in the moon," "When you were sweet sixteen" and other barber-shop quartet favorites of yesteryear died in 1938 at the age of seventy-six. Kerry Mills, whose "Red Wing" is still popular, beat them all by reaching the four-score mark before he died. But those long years did not necessarily bring with them a guarantee of happiness, fame or financial security.

In the early days of his career, James Thornton played in vaudeville with Charles B. Lawlor, another budding song-writer, which brings us to the story of New York City's most famous song. Lawlor, an Irish baritone, sang wherever he could for whatever he could pick up to help balance the family budget.

One sticky hot night in August, 1894, walking home from another singing engagement over on Second Avenue, he saw the tenants of the crowded tenement houses sitting out on the fire escapes looking desperately for a breeze that would never come their way. In the streets, noisy groups of dirty urchins were still hard at play, their parents being loath to call them inside to the dingy, dirty hovels they called home. And way down the street, an organ grinder was hard at work playing for some couples who were too much in love to realize that it was too hot to dance, even in the middle of the street at midnight. Although he had seen the same scene a hundred times, this particular night it began to make a deeper impression upon him than ever before. "New York—what a place," he said to himself as he neared his home. "What a city—big buildings crowding out the sunshine —Manhattan—Brooklyn—Times Square—Broadway—children growing up in the streets—boys and girls dancing the night away—the waltz the old organ grinder is playing—" He soon found himself walking in three-quarter time, and quickly changed his pace as he mounted the steps to the place he called home.

That night the magic and the spell of the big city took possession of Charlie Lawlor. For several hours he tossed restlessly on his bed, reaching out for sleep that always seemed to be just beyond his grasp. Then shortly before dawn he suddenly sat bolt upright in his bed. His wife, startled, said, "Charlie, what's the matter? Are you ill?"

He reached out his hands to reassure her that he was perfectly all right and cried out, "I've got it, honey. I've got a hit!"

"A hit? What kind of a hit? Are you dreaming baseball again?" she asked, anxiously.

Charlie laughed out loud. "No honey; a song hit!" he continued. "I've just thought up the most wonderful idea for a new song all about New York City, and the strains of the loveliest tune keep going through my mind. I'm going to call it, 'The sidewalks of New York.'" Not knowing whether to laugh or cry or call the neighbours, Mrs. Lawlor kept quiet and listened, convinced that she was in the midst of another nightmare of her own. But Charlie kept insisting that he was perfectly sane and absolutely normal.

During breakfast, the composer kept humming the strains of his new waltz tune, trying to pick out appropriate words and phrases to coincide with the rhythm and meter of his music. "I'm going to see Jim Blake," he told his wife when he had hastily downed his second cup of coffee. "He'll know what to do about the words." And with a hasty peck on the cheek that could hardly be called a kiss, out he dashed in search of the neighbourhood poet.

"Jim," he said enthusiastically, "I've got a hit. If you can think up some words as good as my music, we'll really be in the money."

Never one to turn down an opportunity that knocked with such promise, Jim Blake listened to Lawlor's title and tune and then sat down to see what he could do about it. His first efforts were pretty sorry, Lawlor told him, as he urged him to try again. Later that morning he did better, and when Lawlor returned, Jim handed him a piece of paper with a poem which began, "East side, west side, All around the town."

"That's it, Jim," Charlie shouted. "You've done it, lad!"

The next night Charlie introduced the new song in a nearby saloon before the customers had imbibed too freely to know whether the song was good, bad or in-between, and before they were too drunk to care. When they applauded, he went a step further and took it to a music publisher, and, as these stories usually go, it was an immediate success.

The two men, not content to wait out the annual royalty checks, sold their rights for $5,000, split the loot, and called it quits. When the copyright expired after twenty-eight years, Lawlor was smart enough to renew it in his own name, but, since the ditty seemed to have spent itself, he sold his rights a second time for $250.00.

When the big crash came in 1929, Jim Blake lost his job and

just about everything else he owned. Among his cherished souvenirs was a newspaper clipping, now yellowed with age, which contained these lines, "His song has made Jim Blake the idol of New Yorkers, whose city he immortalized. He has but to ask and he has." But Jim was too proud to ask, and, out of a job, hungry, friendless and alone, he died in poverty in 1935, forgotten by the city he had made famous in a song forty-one years before.

When Charlie Lawlor died in 1926 at the age of seventy-three, his song was almost as forgotten as Jim Blake's reputation. But when Al Smith accepted the Democratic Party's nomination for President of the United States, he campaigned with a brown derby in one hand and "The sidewalks of New York" in the other, and the song became more popular than ever before. Now well protected by ASCAP, the royalties began to come in once more, first to the composer's widow, and then, at her death, to their only daughter. Although the song is now public domain, the block-booking of song performance rights will continue to guarantee her further royalties as long as she lives. When informed of this, she said, "Even if I never get another penny from Daddy's song, I know that it will live on." Apparently this was reward enough for the daughter of the man who glamorized the sidewalks of the nation's largest city by capturing something of its life and mood in a high moment of inspiration that humid August night in 1894.

28.

THE STAR SPANGLED BANNER

If it hadn't been for a man with an unusual voice who made a solo out of an anthem, Americans wouldn't have so much trouble reaching the low notes or straining for the high notes of their national song, The Star Spangled Banner.

When John Stafford Smith composed his tune sometime between 1770 and 1775, he wrote it for the new hymn for The Anacreontic Society (named for a Greek poet, Anacreon, who was born in 150 B.C.) which had been written by its president, Ralph Tomlinson; he arranged the composition for four-part male voices. The Society was made up of a group of Londoners devoted to love and wine, who enshrined Venus and Bacchus as their favorite deities. At their meetings, held regularly in the private dining room of the Crown and Anchor Tavern, Strand and Arundel Streets, London, they smoked, sipped drinks, ate bountiful banquets, visited, listened to concerts and invariably sang their own hymn, which began with these lines:

To Anacreon in heaven, where he sat in full glee,
A few sons of harmony sent a petition,
That he their inspirer and patron would be,
And this answer came back from the jolly old Grecian,
"Voice, fiddle and flute, no longer be mute,
I'll lend you my aid and inspire you to boot;
And besides, I'll instruct you, like me, to entwine
The myrtle of Venus with Bacchus' vine."

The baritones and basses would sing the low notes, with the tenors singing the high notes in the middle; all four parts would

116

join in splendid harmony on the last line. And thus was born the tune that was to live as the music for the American national anthem. The music and stanzas appeared in print as early as 1783, and in the composer's "Fifth Book of Canzonets," 1799, it appeared as a four-part anthem. By 1795 it had sung its way across the Atlantic and was widely known in the Colonies. But some nameless soloist set the four-part arrangement aside and sang the whole thing all by himself to the dismay of less gifted singers unto endless generations!

When the "Massachusetts Charitable Fire Society" of Boston commissioned twenty-five-year-old Robert Treat Paine, son of the only clergyman to sign the Declaration of Independence, to compose an original poem to be read at their annual banquet in 1798, the writer naturally turned to the peculiar meter of The Anacreontic Hymn. The young patriot named his poem in honor of the President of the infant Republic, entitling it "Adams and Liberty." He began his nine dramatic stanzas with these majestic words:

Ye sons of Columbia, who bravely have fought
For those rights which unstained from your sires have descended,
May you long taste the blessings your valor has bought,
And your sons reap the soil which their fathers defended.
Mid the reign of mild peace, may your nation increase
With the glory of Rome and the grandeur of Greece;
And ne'er shall the sons of Columbia be slaves
While the earth bears a plant or the sea rolls its waves.

Paine (1773-1811) received $750 for his literary efforts, but was more than repaid when his poem became a patriotic song which was accepted by his fellow-countrymen and widely sung throughout the states to the tune of "The Anacreontic Hymn." After Jefferson's election as third President of the United States, poems appeared under the caption "Jefferson and Liberty." Later, when the Battle of the Wabash, November 4, 1811, made William Henry Harrison famous enough to be elected President, poems in the same unusual meter were written, entitled "The

117

Wabash and Liberty." But all of these were preparatory, although no one realized it at the time. The climax came with the declaration of war by the United States against Great Britain on June 18, 1812, because of the sweeping system of blockade; on the part of the British fleet, designed to cut off French supplies from the United States.

The first two years of this conflict were taken up with land operations in Canada and naval activities on the Great Lakes. The third phase of the war, during its third year, consisted of land and naval operations against the United States proper, and began to get under way early in 1814. On August 14, 1814, British General Ross marched on Washington, D.C. with four thousand picked troops. President and Mrs. Madison fled in the nick of time, finding safety in Charlottesville, Virginia. When the British fleet anchored off Alexandria, Virginia, the capital city surrendered. The British then entered, the soldiers plundering the helpless civilians, taking everything they could lay their hands on.

Dr. William Beanes, an elderly physician of Upper Marlborough, Maryland, was arrested by the British on the ground that he had broken his pledged word not to take up arms against them. The doctor and other Americans had armed themselves against stragglers and plunderers after the main body of British troops had left the city. A mutual friend, Richard West, notified thirty-four-year-old attorney, Francis Scott Key, of Georgetown, that the physician had been taken away by the British. Key, a close friend, received permission from President Madison, upon his return to the capital, to try to effect Dr. Beanes' release. But by that time, the British Admiral had notified James Monroe, Secretary of State, that he intended to sail down the Potomac River, up the Chesapeake Bay, demolish Fort McHenry and destroy not only Baltimore but Washington itself.

Key left his wife with her parents, the Taneys, went to Baltimore, picked up John S. Skinner, captain of a pilot boat on the bay, and arranged to meet the British fleet and release the doctor from their custody. The physician had been kept a prisoner aboard the British frigate "Surprise" for over three weeks, being treated as a common criminal rather than a prisoner of war. Key and Skinner, a government agent for handling flags of truce and exchange of prisoners, found Beanes and arranged for his release. But by that time, Tuesday night and early Wednesday morning, September 13-14, 1814, the British had begun their bombardment of Fort McHenry, gateway to Baltimore. The British put two marines aboard the pilot boat to prevent it from returning to the city. Key's brother-in-law, Judge Joseph H. Nicholson, and a group of volunteers had gone to bolster the defense of the Fort, which was under the command of Major Armistead.

All that fateful night, a huge American flag flying over the scene of battle told the onlookers that the Fort still stood. This flag measured thirty-six feet by twenty-nine feet, bearing fifteen stripes and fifteen stars; at the end of the battle she had been torn by eleven huge bullet holes. The British marines guarding Key, Skinner and Beanes paced the deck anxiously during the night, while the three Americans prayed for a victory they thought well-nigh impossible. But the land attack was repulsed, British General Ross being one of the casualties, and the heavy all-night bombardment destroyed neither the physical defenses nor the spirit of the defenders.

Early Wednesday morning, the British Admiral ordered his fleet to sail back down the bay, at the same time giving Skinner and his two distinguished passengers the right to return to Baltimore. Under the spell of the hour, Key took out a piece of paper and began writing a patriotic poem in the same unusual poetic meter of "The Anacreontic Hymn." His four stanzas began with these lines:

Oh, say, can you see by the dawn's early light
What so proudly we hailed at the twilight's last gleaming?
Whose broad stripes and bright stars, through the perilous fight,
O'er the ramparts we watched were so gallantly streaming!
And the rocket's red glare, the bombs bursting in air
Gave proof through the night that our flag was still there;

Oh, say, does that Star Spangled Banner yet wave
O'er the land of the free and the home of the brave?

The British sailed to New Orleans where their soldiers were again defeated by Andrew Jackson, after a treaty had already been signed at Ghent, Belgium, ending hostilities.

Key, an Episcopalian, "a devout and exemplary man," served as District Attorney for the District of Columbia for three successive terms. In 1857 his book, "Poems of Francis Scott Key" was published. He died in his sixty-third year, January 11, 1843. But the composer of the music lived to see his tune adapted to Paine's poem in 1798 as well as Key's verses in 1814, since he celebrated his eighty-sixth birthday in London in 1836, shortly before his death.

It remained for Herbert Hoover, thirty-first President of the United States, to affix his signature to a law enacted by the Congress, March 3, 1931, reading, "The Star Spangled Banner is designated the national anthem of the United States of America."

29.

THE WRECK OF THE OLD 'NINETY-SEVEN'

One of the three survivors of the famous wreck of the 'Ninety-Seven' that fateful afternoon, September 27, 1903, wasn't even supposed to be on the train at all. When Engineer Joseph "Steve" Broady brought his train to a stop at Lynchburg, Va. enroute from Monroe, Va. to Spencer, N.C., a young express messenger, J. Harris Thompson, jumped aboard to pick up the packages addressed to that office. He had hardly gotten on when the five-car train began tearing down the tracks toward Danville, Va. After all, she was forty-seven minutes late already on her trip from Washington, D.C. to Atlanta, Ga. and Broady, who had taken over the throttle at Monroe, six miles north of Lynchburg, vowed to "put her into Spencer on time."

To maintain her average speed of thirty-seven miles an hour, she had to get up as high as ninety on several grades. But it was worth it, because the little mail train earned more than $140,000 a year for her owners, and if it was speed they wanted, she could furnish it. Although Broady was a veteran of more than twenty years of railroading, he was new on this particular run. When his train went tearing through Gretna Junction a short while later, the frightened telegraph operator whistled and said, " 'Ninety-Seven' is out of control. She must have lost her air brakes."

Usually the train made the one-hundred-sixty-six-mile run from Monroe to Spencer in about four and a quarter hours. But Broady was never one for statistics or figures, even when they warned him to approach Still House Trestle on the outskirts of Danville, Va. at a speed of not more than thirty miles an hour.

That Sunday afternoon, he went down the three-mile grade off White Oak mountain toward the bridge spanning Cherrystone Creek going full blast, with everything wide open. Determined to make up for lost time, he little dreamed that he was "riding into immortality." The bend at his end of the wooden trestle could be negotiated safely only at thirty miles an hour or less. At the last moment, Engineer Broady saw the curve and the citizens of Danville, listening for the familiar long and short toots that heralded the train's arrival, heard instead a long shrill shriek that suddenly became a roar and then was muffled by the sound of crashing timbers climaxed with a series of tremendous thudding shocks as 'Ninety-Seven' plunged off the end of the trestle, thundering to her death in the valley, seventy-five feet below. The first men to reach the scene saw the bodies of the engineer, firemen and conductor lying on the bank of the steep ravine. Of the crew of sixteen, nine were killed instantly, four dying later from their injuries.

Among the three survivors was young Thompson, the unexpected and uninvited passenger from Lynchburg. As the car in which he rode plunged into the ravine, a large safe at one end fell over sideways against the opposite wall, giving him enough protection to escape unscathed from one of the worst and most unnecessary railroad wrecks in American history. As he lay on a mattress on the hillside overlooking the scene of carnage, townspeople came by and asked him, "Is there anything we can do for you? Are you a member of any secret order?" He replied, "No, but if I ever am able to get out of here I'm going to join one if it means that much to so many people." Upon his safe return home, he promptly joined not only the Knights of Pythias but two other lodges.

The leaping train had torn up more than fifty feet of the five-hundred-foot long, seventy-five-foot-high trestle. Wrecking crews were on the site as quickly as they could be mustered, and worked through the night patching up both the trestle and the torn-up track. Shortly after nine o'clock the next morning, trains began to move slowly over that line once more. When curious onlookers inquired about the dozens of little yellow canaries in a grove of pine trees at the top of the ravine, someone explained, "Six crates of those birds were found in the debris caused by the wreck, but not one bird was killed or even injured. In fact, there wasn't a feather out of place in the whole lot. We set them free and there they are, singing for joy at having escaped with their lives."

Among those who happened to be nearby when the wreck occurred was thirty-seven-year-old David Graves George, onetime prize-fighter, revenuer and farmer. Some folks said later that George was impressed by the singing of the canaries which could be heard above the hissing steam of the dying locomotive. Anyway, he was deeply moved, and as soon as he could gather the details of the tragedy, he began writing a ballad about it, singing his words to a tune that sounded a good deal like a familiar mountain tear-jerker, "The ship that never returned." Be that as it may, the ship was soon giving way to the train, and, between the pump house and a barber shop at Gretna (Franklin Junction, Va.) George polished off his new song.

When a recording company began looking for the composer twenty-four years after the wreck that inspired the ballad, so many claimants to the title were discovered that the whole matter was thrown into the courts for settlement. The trials involved would-be authors and singers from Lynchburg, Va. and Greensboro, N.C. as well as a Harvard professor who tried unsuccessfully to solve the riddle all by himself. By the time the case landed in the laps of the nine justices of the United States Supreme Court, more than a million copies of the record, "The Wreck of the Old Ninety-Seven," had been sold, and a sizable sum of money was awaiting the winner, despite trial costs and expenses that had mounted to almost $300,000. The highest judiciary in the land recognized George as the composer, and he was handed a check for $65,295.56 that afternoon in 1935, not bad for an afternoon's composing. Doubtless he raked in more actual cash for less actual work than any composer in the history of music. While Beethoven and Tschaikovsky labored much

123

longer over their immortal symphonies, they didn't realize a fraction of that amount from their magnificent works. But then, maybe they never saw a train wreck, and, anyway they only wrote the music, while the composer of this ballad wrote the words as well.

George lived until Friday, January 23, 1948, when he died in a hospital in Williamsburg, Va. at the age of eighty-two, survived by his widow and fourteen children. He was buried in Forest Lawn Cemetery, Richmond, Va. the following Sunday, in the full knowledge that he had made his contribution to American music, for better or for worse.

30.

THERE'S A LONG LONG TRAIL A-WINDING

"If Hayden and Metz could receive inspiration from a house afire, and Professor Lane could write a hit from the remarks of a sassy waiter, then I can write a song about a painting, "twenty-one-year-old Alonzo Elliott said to his Yale fraternity brothers, one morning in 1913. The boys were examining copies of some famous paintings when the musician of the crowd made his pungent comment.

"What's that about a house afire, Zo?" one of his classmates asked. The young composer replied, "Back in 1886, when Theodore Metz was travelling through the south with the famous McIntyre and Heath Minstrel, the troupe saw a house on fire as they were passing through a small town in Louisiana. McIntyre turned to his fellow comedian and said, 'They're certainly having a hot time in the old town tonight.' Heath passed the expression along to Metz, who composed the tune for which Joe Hayden later wrote the words. The song wasn't published until 1898, during the days of the Spanish-American War, but it became instantly popular. In fact, the American soldiers who went to Cuba sang the song so much that the Cubans thought it was our national anthem. When Teddy Roosevelt's Rough Riders fought at San Juan Hill they sang a different version dealing with the sinking of the battleship 'Maine' by the Spaniards."

"And where does the sassy waiter come in?" another buddy asked.

"Oh, that's a different story," Elliott added. "It couldn't happen at Yale but it did happen at dear old Harvard. A rather shy and retiring Latin teacher named George Martin

125

Lane went into a restaurant near the campus one day to get some lunch. He ordered just one fishball for his noonday meal. When the waiter brought him the lone fishball, Lane asked, 'Where is the bread?' The waiter got mad and shouted, so everyone in the place could hear, 'You get no bread with one fishball.' The poor professor was mortified, but he swallowed his pride and recorded his humiliation in an original song which he called, 'The Lone Fishball.' It was good enough to be printed in Harper's Monthly back in 1855, and became one of the popular songs of the Civil War. That's why I said that if a burning house could inspire 'A hot time in the old town tonight' and a surly waiter could make a dignified professor write a hit song, then I ought to be able to do the same thing with a painting."

The other students gathered around and began to examine the pictures. Elliott pointed to one picture and said, "This is a copy of Jean Meissonier's painting of Napoleon's army cheering the Emperor on the battlefield."

"Who was the painter, Zo?" a curious classmate inquired.

Elliott explained that Jean Louis Ernest Meissonier (1815-1891) was a renowned French painter who specialized in historic, military and genre subjects; he was also France's best-known painter of miniatures. Taking a special liking to Napoleonic subjects, he painted many magnificent canvases, remarkable in their detail, depicting the life and battles of 'The Little Corporal.'

"And what's the name of this one?" another asked.

"That," explained his fraternity brother, "is Meissonier's painting of Napoleon's Retreat from Moscow. Study the picture closely," he continued, "and you'll see the genius of the artist in every stroke of his brush. There is Napoleon astride his famous white horse, Marengo, riding at the head of his retreating forces. You remember the story, don't you? After the crushing defeat of the Austrian forces at Wagram in July 1809, the General gathered an army of nearly half a million men from twenty nations and set forth to subdue the Russians. After weeks of marching, he finally stood on the outskirts of Moscow, on September 14, 1812, only to see the city in flames. The retreating Russians had fired their own city to prevent its capture by the Corsican and had destroyed whatever provisions he had hoped to find within its walls. He couldn't winter his troops in the ruins, so, on October 19, he began his retreat across the frozen, snow-covered steppes back to the security and warmth of his native France. Less than twenty thousand men survived the ordeal, of the magnificent army of nearly five hundred thousand that had advanced across those same plains a few months before. It was a long and lonesome trail homeward for the few who made it. The bravery of Marshal Ney, who commanded the rearguard, prevented an even greater slaughter of the retreating forces."

Later that evening, Alonzo Elliott sat down at the piano in his fraternity house and picked out a tune, with the famous painting in mind. At the urgent request of his fraternity brothers, he sang his new song, "There's a long long trail a-winding," at a banquet a few days later. The boys liked it, but the publishers weren't interested. The following year the youthful composer entered Cambridge University for further study. He wanted a piano for his dormitory room, and shopped in several stores before finding the one he liked. In each store he tried out the instrument by playing his own composition on the keyboard. One dealer was delighted with the new song and urged Elliott to send it to a publisher he knew, but the publisher only filed the manuscript away with dozens of others under "Miscellaneous."

But the boys back at Yale spread the good word far and wide and the new song from New Haven began to catch on with the new generation. When Canadian soldiers disembarked in England during the early years of the first World War, they sang "There's a long long trail" with a zest and enthusiasm that were contagious. The publisher suddenly saw the light, dusted the manuscript off, and started the young Yale graduate on the way to sudden fame. As far as fortune is concerned, he averaged more than $1,000 a year for many years. Eventually the song sold four million copies. Elliott spent most of his money learning how to write greater music. When World War Two ended, he was sixty-one, but he enrolled in the Music Department of the University of New Mexico to work on his Master's degree and to put the finishing touches on an opera based on the life of Billy the Kid.

"Early success can be detrimental," he said, "as it was in my case." But after General Montgomery and his troops marched victoriously across Italy, after having chased Rommel's retreating forces from the sands of North Africa, the bands were playing a new martial air, 'The British Eighth March,' composed in their honor by Alonzo Elliott. From 1913 to 1943 was indeed a long long trail for one who watched two world wars come and go. With the rest of mankind, he earnestly hopes that the long long night of recurrent warfare will soon be over, and that the dreams of peace in every heart will soon come true.

31.

TWINKLE TWINKLE LITTLE STAR

When World War II broke out in 1939, a piece of paper almost a hundred years old was deposited at the British Museum for sakekeeping by the Friends of the National Libraries. Strangely enough, the paper contained a four-line poem written a century earlier by two very remarkable sisters, Jane and Ann Taylor. And long after their hundreds of hymns and poems have been forgotten, children the world over will be repeating those four lines because they comprise one of the best known verses in all the world.

Ann was not only a year older than her talented sister Jane, but also somewhat more gifted. Their father was an engraver in London, England, when Ann was born, January 30, 1782, and also when Jane was born, September 23, 1783. But he later felt the call to the Christian ministry, and joined the Congregational Church, serving as minister in Colchester and later at Ongar. In 1813, when Ann was thirty-one, she married the tutor of mathematics at the Congregational College in Yorkshire, Rev. Joseph Gilbert. When she and her sister began writing poems, they seemed a bit hesitant to invade a field which for too many centuries had been completely dominated by men. In fact, the silence had been broken only twenty-two years before Ann's birth, when Anne Steele (1716-1778) published her book of original hymns and poems in 1760. This unusual volume contained such gems as "Father, whate'er of earthly bliss" and "Father of mercies, in Thy word," and proved that women could do as well as men. Some felt after reading this book that they could beat the men at their own game.

With that encouragement, the Taylor sisters wrote their

hymns and poems, and were elated when several were included in Collyer's "Collection" in 1812, a year prior to the elder sister's marriage. Thirty years later, when Dr. Leifchild edited "Original Hymns," over one hundred poems from the pen of Ann and Jane Taylor were included. The gradual acceptance of women's contributions had earlier inspired the sisters to widen the influence of their writings by publishing them independently. The two girls published "Original Poems" in 1805, following that book with "Hymns for the Nursery" in 1806 and "Hymns for Infant Minds" in 1809. This volume went through more than thirty-five editions. In 1812 they published "Original Hymns for Sunday Schools." The success of their early publications led Ann Gilbert to continue the series, and 1827, three years after Jane's untimely death, saw the publication of two more volumes from her pen and that of her deceased sister, "Hymns for Infant Schools" and "The Wedding Among the Flowers."

Jane began writing maturely in 1804 and her finest works date from that year through 1812. Ann's contributions begin the same year and continued through 1843. After the death of her husband, Ann remained in Nottingham until her own death, in December of 1866. A bit fearful that adults would refuse to sing their hymns, they wrote them with the Sunday School children in mind. In this they adopted the pattern followed successfully a generation later by Cecil Humphreys Alexander (1823-1895) when she prepared her hymns on the phrases of The Apostles' Creed for the children in her Sunday School class. Mrs. Alexander's hymns include such magnificent poems as "There is a green hill far away" and "All things bright and beautiful." Later on they were used more by adults than by the children for whom they were originally created.

The hymns of the Taylor sisters were "marked with directness and simplicity," but they lacked a brightness and warmth for which Christians hungered. Hence they tend to create an atmosphere that is somewhat depressing instead of radiant and joyous. Many of the early women hymn-writers wrote their stanzas from the depths of despair rather than from the heights of victory. Anne Steele began writing after the tragic drowning of her fiance the day before their scheduled wedding. And Harriet Auber (1773-1862), a contemporary of the Taylors, wrote her first outstanding hymn under the gloomy premonition that her sweetheart would not return from the Napoleonic Wars to make her his bride. He was slain in the Battle of Waterloo sometime after she had scratched out her first great hymn with the diamond of her engagement ring on the window pane of her home. It was the poem beginning, "Our blest Redeemer, ere He breathed His tender last farewell." Under some such cloud, the Taylors wrote their hymns and may be excused for shrouding some of their sentiments with a pall of gloom, since that seemed to be the habit of the times in which they lived and wrote. Thus it is even more remarkable that the two sisters should have dashed off the four lines that will endear them to children for all time to come.

John Keats had not yet written his poem "On Reading Chapman's Homer" which contains these lines, "Then felt I like some watcher of the skies When a new planet swims into his ken," when Ann and Jane Taylor stood out under the starry heavens one clear night, and "returned the stare of the stars." Little did they dream that the light they saw twinkling from the heavens had been travelling at an unbelievable rate of speed for so many centuries and even millennia.

"The stars are twinkling like diamonds," Ann said to her sister.

"Like the diamond in your engagement ring or the diamond with which Harriet scratched out her first poem on the window pane," Jane added.

"I wonder if there is life on those planets or any of those stars," Ann continued. "Maybe I should ask, What is a star anyway? Is it a flaming sun so far away that we can only see it? Does it bring the same light and warmth and life to other earths that our sun brings to us? Surely 'the heavens declare the glory of God'; surely the Psalmist was right when he said,

'When I consider thy heavens, the moon and the stars which thou hast ordained, What is man that thou art mindful of him, and the son of man that thou visitest him.' "

"We should write a verse for our Sunday School collection about the twinkling stars," Jane suggested.

"Excellent, Jane," her sister answered. And before they went in that night they had written these four lines with which their names will be forever linked and their memories forever hallowed:

Twinkle, twinkle little star, How I wonder what you are, Up above the world so high, Like a diamond in the sky.

And it was that poem that friends entrusted to the safe-keeping of the British Museum when the world came crashing down in ruin at the outbreak of the second World War. Fortunately, the stars are not affected by our mundane rivalries and conflicts, and will continue to twinkle in the sky as constant reminders of God's watchful care over the children He is pleased to call His own.

32.

WAIT TILL THE SUN SHINES, NELLIE *

The president of the largest popular music company in the United States told this writer recently that in 1954 there were more than fifty-three thousand new songs copyrighted in the Copyright Division of the Library of Congress. Of that number his company examined more than thirteen thousand and finally published less than three hundred.

But Harry Von Tilzer, popular song giant of yesteryear, used to say, "There are one hundred and forty million people in the United States, all of them song-writers." And he should know, because as a composer and publisher of note he met up with the well-knowns, and the has-beens as well as the never-weres of the song publishing game.

When he came out of the middle west to invade and capture New York City in 1892, he was just plain Harry Gumm. Before setting out to beard the musical lions in their dens he decided to do something about that name. He liked his mother's maiden name, Tilzer, so he discarded his own for hers, adding the "Von," he later confessed, to give the new name "class." This was by no means the first time a musician and composer sought to enhance his chances of success by doctoring up his name, but few have had the good fortune to select one as imposing as Harry's.

Several decades earlier, a famous Philadelphian by the name of Septimus Winner (1827-1902) adopted the name of Alice Hawthorn as his pen-name, following the trend made famous by the French woman of letters, Amandine Lucile Aurore

---

* The song title of this story is copyrighted by the Harry Von Tilzer Music Publishing Co.

Dupin, who used the male pen-name, George Sand. While some pious people thought that "Whispering Hope" was the composition of a saintly, dignified old lady, steeped in Christian culture and reeking with sanctimoniousness, brother Winner was laughing up his sleeve. In addition to his success with sacred songs, Septimus (was he the seventh child of his parents?) won further laurels with sentimental ballads. One day in 1854, half a century before Von Tilzer appeared on the scene, he heard Whistling Dick Milburn, a Negro guitar player and entertainer, whistling a new tune. Before long, Winner had written his own words to the tune that came to him almost ready made, and gave to the world the haunting strains of "Listen to the mockingbird" and a generation of girls named "Hallie." While the chances are that Winner (or Hawthorn (you choose your sex and take your choice) never actually heard a mockingbird singing, it is no stranger than the fact that Jack Norworth, who wrote "Take me out to the ball game" in 1906 never actually saw a major league ball game until many many years after he wrote his big league hit! He commented on that fact in these words, "There is nothing strange about a song-writer not knowing about what he writes."

It was Lottie Gilson, the comic opera star, who encouraged Von Tilzer to pack up his bags, pick up his music and head for the great white way. So he arrived in New York with a pile of unpublished songs, $1.65 in cash and the determination to make America listen to his songs and then take them to its heart as its very own. The first few years were tough ones. Like other undiscovered artists, he sang for meals, as well as for pennies and dollars, and sold his new songs for whatever they would bring. As his fame grew he demanded as much as $15 for an original composition, quite a jump from the $2 fee he collected when he began singing at Tony Pastor's. But he had what it took, and soon little old New York was patting its feet to the beat of his songs and crying for more of the same.

He tried his hand at composing some novelty tunes with a sheet of paper placed between the hammers and strings of his piano. "It gives the music an orchestral effect," he explained to a newspaper reporter friend, Monroe Rosenfield. But Monroe couldn't see it that way, because, try as he might, the piano didn't sound like the Philharmonic Symphony! Finally he shouted, "What kind of a tin pan do you call that?" Von Tilzer laughed and kept pounding the keys. "This street must sound like a tin pan alley with so many pianos making such a din," he replied, coining the phrase by which the music publishing section of Broadway is known to this day.

New York may mean Ebbets Field or Yankee Stadium to the sportsman, Rockefeller Center to the tourist, Lewishon Stadium and Julliard to the long-hairs, Columbia University to the intellectual and Riverside Church or the Cathedral of St. John the Divine to the Christian, but to the song-writer it means "Tin Pan Alley."

The inspiration for his big hit came so suddenly that a less attentive person would have let it slip right through his fingers. In 1905 he was sitting in the lobby of a hotel in his adopted city, talking with a well-known writer of lyrics, Andrew Stirling. Looking around the lobby during a lull in the conversation, his eyes fell upon a lovely young bride who was crying as if her heart would break. He saw a young man put his arm about her, trying to comfort her, and he wondered what she was weeping about. Cocking an ear in their direction, he heard her say, "But you promised to take me to Coney Island. I've been looking forward to that all my life. And now it's raining." The young man, obviously her groom, did his best to explain that the rain was not his fault. "I'll take you some other time, Nellie," Von Tilzer heard him say. "As soon as the weather clears, we'll go. I promise you. Just wait till the sun shines, Nellie." She took his arm in hers and together they walked slowly back to their room.

Von Tilzer had heard enough. Before the day was over he had written "Wait Till the Sun Shines, Nellie," one of the

135

most famous of his more than five thousand popular songs. The English song-writer, Harry Decker, had had a similar experience in the 1880s. Landing in New York, he complained to the Customs Officer about the duty he was forced to pay for a bicycle he had brought with him. "You're lucky it isn't a bicycle built for two," a fellow song-writer, Billy Jerome, commented. Decker had heard enough and "A Bicycle Built for Two" will be sung long after the vehicle itself has become a museum piece and the singers gad about in their fancy convertibles or cruise off into the heavens in their space ships.

Before he died at seventy-three, Von Tilzer had composed such perennial favorites as "I want a girl," "A bird in a gilded cage" and "Rufus Rastus Johnson Brown." In addition, he had encouraged other composers by publishing their music and introducing it to the public. Two of those whom he started on the road he himself had trod were George Gershwin and Irving Berlin. Through his gift of music, he has made the sun shine through many a cloudy sky for many Nellies and their sweethearts, who will continue to make his lilting songs the channels by means of which they will express their own feelings toward those whom they love.

33.

WAY DOWN UPON THE SWANEE RIVER

The only man ever to write two songs which were later adopted by two different states as their "official songs" turned to his brother and said, "The word Pedee isn't romantic enough, and heaven knows Mississippi and Missouri are much too long. The river I want must have only two syllables. Look in the geography book or the atlas over there on the shelf and see what you can find."

Twenty-five-year-old Stephen Collins Foster was just about through with his new song, and the magic name of the right river was all he needed to complete it. His brother looked through the geography book and studied the maps of the several states rather closely. "Say, Stephen, how about Okefenokee? That's the name of a big swamp in Florida."

"Goodness, no," the composer shouted. "That's as bad as Tallahassee. Get out of those Indian names and find something with two syllables."

His brother studied the map again and then said, "Stephen, here's a river that would fit, but it has three syllables instead of two."

"What is it?" the musician asked.

"Suwannee," his brother answered.

"Not bad at that," Stephen commented. "We could cut out the 'Su' part of it and make up a new name, Swanee. Let me try it out on the piano." Seating himself at the keyboard, Foster struck a chord and began to sing, "Way down upon the Pedee River," and then began again with this line, "Way down upon the Swanee River."

His brother interrupted. "Excellent," he said. "That will do fine. Swanee, Pedee. Yes; Swanee is perfect."

"It suits me better than any other so far. Let's write it down and call it quits," the youthful musician added. That afternoon in 1851 the young man who was to be known in future years as America's favorite song-writer put the finishing touches on the song he called "Old folks at home," without ever having seen the river he immortalized in its lilting lines. While he would have considered himself the last man on earth ever to write a state song, Florida not only dedicated in his honor five of the bridges that cross the Suwannee River, but selected his song as the official state song. Today a Stephen Foster Memorial Park, complete with carillon, amphitheatre and statue of the composer, is being developed on the banks of the river that was fortunate enough to have a name that could be cut down to two syllables. Foster proudly signed his name to the new composition as both author and composer.

This was a far cry from the day, six years earlier, when a big minstrel troupe had come to Pittsburgh, the young musician's home. Born in Lawrenceville, now a part of the western Pennsylvania metropolis, on July 4, 1826, the young composer early peddled his songs to any and every attentive audience, be it large or small. The members of the minstrel liked one of his numbers, a song entitled "Oh Susanna," and decided to add it to their repertoire. That was four years before it became the favorite of the forty-niners in the mad rush to California after gold was discovered at Sutter's Mill. A bit hesitant to sign his name to the song, he asked Edward P. Christy, the owner of the travelling entertainers, to list it as one of his own compositions. He didn't want his musical reputation to suffer by associating himself with a ditty as simple as "Oh Susanna."

Later when the popularity of his songs convinced him that it was no dishonor to be known as a minstrel song-writer, or an "Ethiopian composer," he proudly let the world know that Stephen Foster was the composer of "Massa's in de cold cold ground," "Jeanie with the light brown hair," written for the one great love of his life, Jane McDowell, whom he married in 1850, "Old dog tray," "Camptown Races," "Nelly was a lady," "Gentle Annie," "Come where my love lies dreaming," and dozens of other sacred and sentimental selections.

"Old folks at home" sold more than two hundred thousand copies, bringing in the composer only about $1,700 in royalties.

The chiefly self-taught musician had early given signs of a remarkable artistic career. He learned to play the flageolet when only seven; at fourteen he composed a waltz for four flutes and in 1842, at sixteen, he published his first song, "Open thy lattice, love." He immortalized an old stately mansion near Bardstown, Kentucky in "My Old Kentucky Home," which that state adopted as its official state song, giving Foster the honor of having composed the state songs of Florida and Kentucky, a privilege denied any other American composer to the present time.

But the close of his life was as fraught with tragedy as his early years had been filled with promise. His simple melodies touched the hearts of the American people who quickly made them their very own. He had the gift of expressing the sentiments which everyone holds dear, and setting those ideas to music that everyone could easily sing.

A few days after he had composed his last successful song, "Beautiful Dreamer," in 1864, his thirty-eighth year, and plagued with the curse of drink that had haunted him for more than a decade, he was found lying half-naked and bleeding from a bad wound in his neck, in the hallway of a cheap rooming house in the Bowery. In the desperate journey either to find himself or run away from himself, he had deserted his friends and loved ones. When he was carried to New York's Bellevue Hospital by the police, no one knew who he was or where he came from. In one pocket they found only thirty-eight cents, and in another a scrap of paper bearing these plaintive words, "Dear friends and gentle hearts," the title for an unwritten song. Not until two weeks later was the account of his death carried in the newspapers. Apparently few knew and none cared.

So died the northern boy who caught the romance and glamor of the old south in his songs long before he ever travelled below the Mason and Dixon line, and became the nation's most beloved troubadour. Had he not succumbed to alcoholic drink, what greater songs could he not have written, or did he seek solace in the bottle because he had written himself out too soon?

The Stephen Collins Foster Memorial Building on the campus of the University of Pittsburgh honors the gifted song-writer, not for the delirium he suffered in his later years, but for the delight he gave to his native land in the charming songs of his earlier and happier years.

34.

WHEN IRISH EYES ARE SMILING

Some of the sorriest songs turn out to be the biggest financial successes, while some of the greatest composers go half-starved and half-naked to meet their Creator. And money seems to pour in on those who are not professional musicians and composers, but who use the cash merely to supplement what they earn in other, more lucrative fields.

For example, Hollywood actor Gene Lockhart makes a good living playing in the movies, but a song he wrote in collaboration with Ernest Seitz in 1919 continues to pay off year after year, because it is the ever popular "The world is waiting for the sunrise."

If the unknown composer of "Chopsticks," which was first published in Glasgow, Scotland in 1877, had copyrighted his music and collected royalties on its use, he would have become almost a millionaire, because his tune turned out to be the most famous "one-finger" composition of that age as well as our own.

The Inquiring Photographer Jimmy Jemail once asked a Tin Pan Alley song-writer this question, "How do you get your inspiration for your songs? Billy Hill, a struggling composer, took the newspaperman to his home. The place was cold and damp because the musician owed a gas bill of $36 and the company had cut off their supply pending payment, while his wife was about to become a mother. "There's the real inspiration," the composer said; "I need the money." Some hours later, Hill turned out three songs which he offered a reputable publisher for the $36 he needed to pay the overdue gas bill. The business man laughed, but Hill had the last laugh because another publisher bought them and made a killing on two of the three, "The old spinning wheel" and "The last roundup," quite a contrast to the million bucks the writers of "The prisoner's song" were said to have amassed from their composition.

George Graft Jr., according to a news item that appeared some years ago, claimed to have written "When Irish eyes are smiling" in 1912, in collaboration with two other men. In "financial straits" at the time, the composers assigned that song and "sixty-eight other songs" to the M. Whitmark and Sons Publishing Company of New York City, in 1917, realizing $1,600.00. Commenting on that later, the composer added, "That meant we got an average of $23 for each song." The publisher then proceeded to copyright all of the songs in his own name, a standard procedure in the music publishing game. When the time came for the copyrights to be renewed twenty-eight years later to cover the second twenty-eight year period the law allows, both the composer and the company applied for the renewal. That created a problem, to say the least. The composer insisted that he had the right to renew the copyright, which was limited entirely and completely to him and/or his family, while the company insisted with equal vehemence that it was their privilege and not the composer's. When the United States Supreme Court finally got around to considering the case in all of its complexities and ramifications, it disagreed with the musician and decreed in favor of the company. One Justice did not participate in the ruling, while three dissented. So, out of the 'nine old men,' five said "No" to the composer and "Yes" to the publisher, a pretty narrow margin of victory on which to establish a legal precedent. Undoubtedly the composer's eyes were not smiling at the thought of the money the publisher was making and would make on his song. But then maybe he had never been to Ireland in the first place to see the original "smiling eyes of the ould sod" in their native setting! That would even up the score, to some extent.

As far as money is concerned, it was a humiliated composer

who lost his wallet while on a Parisian honeymoon. It was more embarrassing when the waiter in the Cafe Maxim refused to believe him and took him straight to the manager. But the older man believed the young husband's tale of woe and not only wrote off the expense of the dinner but loaned him the money with which to purchase two tickets back to their home in Vienna. "You will never regret your generosity," the young man replied. The manager smiled, and wished them both God-speed on their journey and many years of happiness together, little dreaming that he would ever be repaid for his kindness.

But years later the owners of the Cafe Maxim had reason to thank the gracious manager for his hospitality to the young Viennese couple, because the young man was Franz Lehar, and when he put the finishing touches on the music of "The Merry Widow," he included the Cafe Maxim song, and the proprietor suddenly found himself managing the most famous night club in the gay French capital.

Whether future Congressman Thomas Dunn English ever collected a penny for his most popular poem has never been ascertained. He served in the House of Representatives from 1891 to 1895 "neither framing famous measures nor delivering powerful speeches." However, his claim to fame does not rest on his political laurels but on a sad and melancholy bit of verse he wrote almost half a century before he went to Washington as a freshman law-maker, the poem which begins with the question, "Do you remember sweet Alice, Ben Bolt?" The journals English later edited went bankrupt and the dramas he wrote were played to empty theatres before folding up. But while he lost money on his literary ventures, he won the respect and admiration of his fellow Americans by the sad story of a girl named Alice "who wept with delight when you gave her a smile, And trembled with fear at your frown."

Such are the shifting fortunes of the song writing business. Even J. S. Fearis, who wrote the music of the gospel song, "Beautiful isle of somewhere," could comment on the irony of the situation. A little ditty he dashed off one day for some children in the neighbourhood later earned more money for a radio singer and a swing band than the musician ever realized from all of his compositions, because one of the girl scouts who learned the new song, "Little Sir Echo," remembered it when she grew up, and passed it on to a band leader, who recorded the "Echo Song," and, with her help, went on to make a fair sized pile of money on it.

The simplest songs suddenly capture the public fancy and sweep the country like a prairie fire, while some of the finest songs gather dust for generations, finally earning for those who plug and promote them the fortunes which were denied their creators.

35.

YANKEE DOODLE

The fourth war between France and England for possession of North America began in 1754. Previously the two European powers had grappled for the wealth of the new world three times between 1689 and 1748, but the issue was still unsettled. This fourth conflict saw the French lining up with the Indians, while the British allied themselves with the American colonists in what is known as "The French and Indian War." George Washington's expedition to capture the French post, Fort Duquesne, on the site where the modern city of Pittsburgh stands, had been a failure. General Braddock's ill-fated march into the wilderness toward the same objective likewise met with dismal defeat, the General himself being one of the casualties of the campaign.

Early in 1755, a small detachment of British and American soldiers was stationed at Fort Crailo, the site of the famous Van Rensselaer home across the Hudson River from present-day Albany, New York. During the evenings of the late spring and early summer, the soldiers would sit and chat about the well just back of the imposing and easily-defended manor house. Although they were allies in war, there was little love lost between the brilliantly-trained, well-armed British troops and the poorly-trained and ill-equipped American soldiers. What they said of each other behind their respective backs is unprintable. And what their enemies, the French, had to say about them both was of the same calibre.

Of course, the French called the British many things, among them the word for English in the French language, "L'anglais." That word puzzled their Indian allies no end. They couldn't pronounce the word in the first place and they hadn't the slightest idea what it meant, in the second place. But they did the best they could, and got the idea that the Britishers were "langlais," or, as some tribes finally pronounced it, "yangee." By the time the new word spread through the numerous Indian nations engaged in the war, it had become an entirely different word, "yankee."

Naturally the red men thought the word applied only to the white men in that section of the country, so soon they were calling all Britishers and Americans yankees. The British resented the fact that the Americans were beating them at their own game, and were galled at being called "yankees" along with their allies.

After all, the British had the finest army in the world. Strictly adhering to the traditions that had made them great, they marched to fight the Indians as they had fought the Germans and French for years. The Indians aimed their arrows at the red bands across the English chests, and soon there was a dead Englishman for every Indian arrow. Still they refused to discard their fancy uniforms, even if it meant losing battles and sacrificing good men needlessly.

The Americans, on the other hand, looked like the woods where they lived and even smelled like the animals they shot for their food and clothing. And they fought the Indian as the Indian fought them, and gradually began to win battles despite the nondescript tactics they employed. If it had to be "every man for himself," then they fought that way, having no military traditions to hold them back. This galled their allies more and more.

"I don't know whether we're on the right or wrong side of this war," one British soldier said to his comrades one night. "If I had my way, I'd fight with the French against the Americans instead of with the Americans against the French. After all, the French have some culture, but these crude Americans—bah!"

The British regimental surgeon, Dr. Richard Shuckburg,

146

walked up about that time. "I agree with you men," he said. "These Americans aren't supposed to fight successfully, but they do. I'll take them as comrades at arms, but never as my equals. They are as headstrong, stubborn and wild a bunch of soldiers as has ever shouldered a musket. As for culture, they don't even know the word, much less its meaning."

"Then let's show them up for the ignoramuses they are," another suggested.

"How?" still another asked. The first man looked up at the physician. "What about it, Doc? What can we do?"

The physician thought for a moment and then replied. "The Americans don't sing. They have no music. We have a noble musical tradition in England, but these poor fools don't know what a song is," he continued.

"What are you getting at, Doc?" a soldier asked.

"Just this," the doctor replied. "Let's make up a silly song and then palm it off on these dumb Americans as a famous European marching song. They don't have any better sense than to believe us and take it up. And while they're singing it, we can laugh up our sleeves at them and they'll never know the difference."

The soldiers were enthusiastic. "Excellent," several said.

The upshot of it all was that that very same evening around the well at Fort Crailo, the British soldiers and their regimental surgeon dreamed up a ditty about a Yankee half-wit, which they called "Yankee Doodle," since a "doodle" was a half-wit, as everyone knew. A sillier song would be hard to find in the annals of music, foreign or domestic. But they wrote several printable stanzas to a tune that was said to come from a Dutch buttermilk festival and when the Americans returned from a foray into the woods, their allies graciously consented to teach them the famous European marching song.

The Americans, not knowing any better, learned the song and liked it. Because they had nothing else to sing, they soon began to add stanzas too numerous to mention, accepting the song for what their British comrades insisted it actually was.

147

By 1775 when the Americans were fighting for their own independence against their former allies, they made "Yankee Doodle" their marching song in reality. In 1871, when Cornwallis surrendered to Washington at Yorktown, everyone was singing it. Cornwallis remarked, "I am thoroughly bored with the song and hope that I never have to hear it again," sentiments with which his conquerors concurred!

A group of idle rich young Englishmen toured Italy one summer, and were introduced to spaghetti and macaroni. They took to the macaroni, and, upon their return to England, sat around in cafes and taverns eating macaroni. Soon the word "macaroni" came to designate a type of lazy, widely-travelled, wealthy, well-dressed ne'er-do-wells, who affect foreign ways. When the American soldiers saw their British allies all dressed up in their fancy colorful uniforms, they dubbed them "macaronies." And one enterprising Yankee shot a turkey, stuck its feathers in his cap and said, "I'm just as macaroni as any of them!" Which gave rise to the puzzling verse that says:

> Yankee Doodle came to town, Riding on a pony,
> Stuck a feather in his cap and called it 'macaroni.'

Though many poets have labored to improve the original stanzas, the song remains today just as it was at the close of the French and Indian War; and it became the first famous patriotic song in American history.

INDEX